THE HIGHLY SENSITIVE CHILD

2 Books In 1

How Conscious Parents Can Help Their Children
Overcome the Challenges This Trait Imposes
+
Age By Age Strategies Birth to Age 20

Laura Henry x Royal Owl Books

This Book Includes

Book 1:
PARENTING A HIGHLY SENSITIVE CHILD
Raised With Adequate Understanding and Care
Can Our Children Become Strong, Aware,
and Well-Adjusted Adults

Book 2:
THE HIGHLY SENSITIVE CHILD FROM CHILDHOOD TO ADOLESCENCE
A Comprehensive Guide Addressing The Needs Of
Specific Age Groups Birth to Age 20

© Copyright 2021 by Royal Owl Books - All rights reserved.

The following Book is reproduced below with the goal of providing information that is as accurate and reliable as possible. Regardless, purchasing this Book can be seen as consent to the fact that both the publisher and the author of this book are in no way experts on the topics discussed within and that any recommendations or suggestions that are made herein are for entertainment purposes only. Professionals should be consulted as needed prior to undertaking any of the action endorsed herein.

This declaration is deemed fair and valid by both the American Bar Association and the Committee of Publishers Association and is legally binding throughout the United States.

Furthermore, the transmission, duplication, or reproduction of any of the following work including specific information will be considered an illegal act irrespective of if it is done electronically or in print. This extends to creating a secondary or tertiary copy of the work or a recorded copy and is only allowed with the express written consent from the Publisher. All additional right reserved.

The information in the following pages is broadly considered a truthful and accurate account of facts and as such, any inattention, use, or misuse of the information in question by the reader will render any resulting actions solely under their purview. There are no scenarios in which the publisher or the original author of this work can be in any fashion deemed liable for any hardship or damages that may befall them after undertaking information described herein.

Additionally, the information in the following pages is intended only for informational purposes and should thus be thought of as universal. As befitting its nature, it is presented without assurance regarding its prolonged validity or interim quality. Trademarks that are mentioned are done without written consent and can in no way be considered an endorsement from the trademark holder.

Table Of Contents

PARENTING A HIGHLY SENSITIVE CHILD

INTRODUCTION

CHAPTER 1: WHAT IS HIGHLY SENSITIVE?

CHAPTER 2: HOW TO DETERMINE IF A CHILD IS HIGHLY SENSITIVE

CHAPTER 3: PREJUDICES ABOUT THE HIGHLY SENSITIVE CHILD

CHAPTER 4: HOW TO EXPLAIN TO OTHERS THAT THE HIGHLY SENSITIVE CHILD IS NEITHER CAPRICIOUS NOR TOO SHY

CHAPTER 5: HOW TO DISTINGUISH BETWEEN A HIGHLY SENSITIVE CHILD AND REAL DISORDERS

CHAPTER 6: THE SITUATION IN WHICH PARENTS ARE HSP

CHAPTER 7: THE SITUATION IN WHICH PARENTS ARE NOT HSP

CHAPTER 8: HOW TO BE A CAPABLE PARENT TO A HIGHLY SENSITIVE CHILD

CHAPTER 9: DEVELOPING THE PARENTING SKILLS NEEDED TO HELP AN HSC GROW UP

CHAPTER 10: SECRETS TO RAISING A HAPPY HSC

CHAPTER 11: THE JOY OF RAISING AN HSC

CHAPTER 12: TIPS AND RULES FOR PARENTS OF HIGHLY SENSITIVE CHILDREN

CHAPTER 13: STRATEGIES TO SUPPORT AND CALM YOUR CHILD

CHAPTER 14: FIFTEEN STRATEGIES FOR PARENTING A SENSITIVE CHILD

CHAPTER 15: WHAT SHOULD OUR APPROACH BE TO HSCS?

CHAPTER 16: HOW DO YOU DEAL WITH A SENSITIVE CHILD?

CHAPTER 17: ADVICE FOR PARENTS OF HIGHLY SENSITIVE CHILDREN

CONCLUSION

THE HIGHLY SENSITIVE CHILD FROM CHILDHOOD TO ADOLESCENCE

INTRODUCTION

CHAPTER 1: WHAT IS HIGH SENSITIVITY

CHAPTER 2: HOW TO RECOGNIZE A HIGHLY SENSITIVE CHILD AND CARE FOR HIM OR HER

CHAPTER 3: TIPS IF YOUR NEWBORN CRIES TOO MUCH

CHAPTER 4: 2 TO 6 MONTHS

    Tips on How to Manage Overstimulation
    Tips on How to Manage Sleep Problems
    What Kind of Sleep Does a Baby Need?

CHAPTER 5: 1 TO 5 YEARS. PRE-SCHOOL AGE. AT HOME

    Managing HSC at Home
    Encourage the Reflective Nature of the HSC

CHAPTER 6: 1 TO 5 YEARS. PRE-SCHOOL. OUTSIDE THE HOME

    How to Support the HSC When Entering the World
    Social Shyness, Trying New Things, Kindergarten

CHAPTER 7: HSC AGES 5 AND 12. IN SCHOOL-AGE. AT HOME AND OUT OF HOME

    Give HSC Social Skills to Live in the World
    Get the HSC to Talk to Parents, an Adult, or a Psychiatrist
    In the Shadows of Our Words

CHAPTER 8: HSC AGES 14 TO 20. TEENS

    How to Handle a Highly Sensitive Adolescent
    Accept the Adolescent's Need to Distance Themselves From Their Parents
    Help in Coping With High School
    Sexuality for an HSC
    Healthy Communication
    Why HSCs Benefit from Social Media Detoxes
    Dealing with Anxiety as an HSC
    Erikson's Theories

CONCLUSION

PARENTING A HIGHLY SENSITIVE CHILD

Raised With Adequate Understanding and Care
Can Our Children Become Strong, Aware,
and Well-Adjusted Adults

Laura Henry x **Royal Owl Books**

Introduction

In the 1980s, Dr. Elaine Aron coined the term 'highly sensitive person" to describe a person who is more aware or responsive to emotional, physical, and other stimuli than the average person. She noticed that many of her patients exhibited traits such as being easily startled, quick to cry or laugh, easily overwhelmed by things like bright lights or loud noises, and not being good at masking those reactions. It's been three decades since she first published her findings on what she calls a trait that's both common and misunderstood, but in recent years, Aron has observed that children are becoming increasingly sensitive as well.

A sensitive child is not an unruly or undisciplined child. They are not shy but they find it hard to deal with the physical, social, and emotional demands of school life. They are not weak or lacking in self-esteem, but they experience the world around them as intense and overwhelming. When you add to that the pressure from parents and teachers to do better, be better, it's a recipe for a highly-strung child who can easily become anxious, physically ill, and in some cases even depressed at a young age.

Aron is now seeing more of these highly sensitive children in her practice, as well as the adults who were once those children. She says the term 'highly sensitive' has evolved to mean more than just being on the sensitive side of the bell curve, and while her original research focused on adult patients with a diagnosis of childhood disorders such as autism, she's discovered that many of her clients can also be perfectly healthy.

Aron is careful to point out that becoming a 'sensitive' child is not an illness or a sign that your child always needs to be taken care of. Anyone can have an overly sensitive personality, but Aron sees it as something parents should be aware of. While you don't have to be afraid of your child or constantly coddle them, they do need more understanding and support. Recognizing that your child is highly sensitive can help you to be more understanding and supportive, says Aron.

While there's no universal definition of what it means to be a highly sensitive person, the trait is actually seen in 20% of the population. It's not gender-specific, and although it has been found to run in families, it doesn't mean you need to be born with it or have a parent or sibling who is also highly sensitive. There are very few professionals who have heard of it or know what to do with it, except for a small number of emotional therapists and counselors. Schools, employers, and healthcare professionals are not trained to deal with people who are sensitive, especially children.

To be classified as highly sensitive, Aron says your child needs to score high on at least five out of the nine traits she has identified. These include:

•   They need more time to process information than the average person.

•   They become over-stimulated by strong sensory stimuli such as bright lights, loud noises, and strong smells.

•   They are easily over-aroused or under-aroused and have a hard time calming down.

•   They need to talk themselves down' from being overwhelmed by strong emotions as they are more likely to feel physical symptoms such as a racing heart, sweaty palms, or nausea when exposed to strong feelings.

•   They tend to be highly reactive, feel things more deeply, can become overwhelmed very easily, and require more reassurance than most people.

While the traits of highly sensitive children are seen in some adults as well, Aron says her research suggests these traits are most likely found in children due to hormonal changes during the sensitive period of early childhood. She identifies that the time between birth and the age of three is critical for the development of those traits.

The most important thing to do is to provide a stable environment for your child, says Aron. Highly sensitive children have a hard time coping with instability or changes and will likely respond in one of three ways:

•	They become withdrawn and may feel so overwhelmed by their emotions that they can't cope with what's happening around them.

•	They become over-reactive, which means they react to even small things out of proportion to the actual stimulus.

•	They become overly anxious, which means they are constantly looking for reassurance from others and they can be easily triggered by even minor changes in their surroundings.

The trait of being highly sensitive may not be something you noticed about your child until he or she was much older, but Dr. Aron says there are some ways to recognize it in an infant. Highly sensitive children:

•	Are easily soothed by gentle talking and touch.

•	Are calmed by performing a familiar routine, such as saying 'night-night.'

•	Are disturbed by changes in routine or being in new places.

•	Cry easily when hungry, tired, or overstimulated.

- Respond to the feelings of other people around them. For example, if one of their siblings is crying, they may cry too without having any idea why the other child is upset.

- Are responsive to gentle play like looking at books with bright pictures or stickers and are particularly attracted to interactive books that talk, light up, or play music like Sesame Street books and toys.

Try to keep things as regular as possible. For example, food should be a part of their routines, not something new or unpredictable that can upset them during the sensitive period.

If they don't sleep much at night, it may mean that they are especially sensitive to sounds and noises in their environment while they are sleeping.

Another thing you can do if you're noticing signs your child is highly sensitive is to take them out into nature for an hour each day. Being in nature gives them a sense of calm and familiarity where they do not have the same sensory stimuli and overwhelming emotions as they do at home, says Aron.

CHAPTER 1:

What Is Highly Sensitive?

One of the pioneers in understanding the attribute of these people is Dr. Elaine Aron. She led research and came out with a book called "The Highly Sensitive Person," laying out the attributes of these kinds of individuals. Through her broad examination, Dr. Aron had the option to help many individuals in understanding themselves with this normal, but not very talked-about, personality attribute of being sensitive. Her work has brought forth other exploration as numerous individuals were more interested in the subject and how individuals with this condition can be drawn closer.

Regarding pervasiveness, Dr. Aron says that around 20% of the populace is considered "highly sensitive." At a significant rate, they are viewed as typical, however, not pervasive. This is critical to note because the standard comprehension of HSP is that being too sensitive is a sickness or turmoil that should be relieved and be freed of. Highly sensitive individuals might be viewed as "excessively timid," "high support," "excessively critical," or just irrationally sensitive. The board of these people has been coordinated to a clinical methodology, as though being too sensitive can disappear with a couple of pills. This is a gross misconception of what being a Highly Sensitive Person is. A reductive and limited sort of reasoning like this may hurt them in the short and long run. They are a typical piece of our populace even though they may not fit the more mainstream or normal personality attributes we are aware of.

A Highly Sensitive Person is somebody who has an elevated feeling of their environmental factors, who shows solid reactivity to inside and outside boosts, who has expanded passionate connectedness, and who has an inclination to turn inwards. This definition might be hard to see; however, we can unload these characteristics individually. Remember, individuals you may realize who have this or notice your children on the off chance that you feel that they show some of these practices.

They give close consideration to inside and outside boosts. These individuals have tactile receptors which can get considerably more sensation than typical individuals. This doesn't allude to any anatomical overabundance. They are not individuals with more eyes, more noses, more ears, or a larger number of receptors in their skin than the ordinary populace. Instead, these individuals have receptors that are more sensitive to improvements. Their faculties are more increased in most people.

For instance, they can be specific to the smell of their environmental factors.

If typical individuals go to a room without seeing anything, they may get certain scents that may not be clear.

Regarding contact, they can be extremely specific to skin sensations. Regarding clothing, some even create hypersensitive responses to specific sorts of textures. They can be fastidious in what sort of clothing they wear because the clothing would be invigorating their body the entire time they are worn. Contact incorporates temperature. Highly Sensitive Persons are more sensitive to temperature changes, either feeling too cold or too hot when the rest might not say anything negative. The response might be showed dermatologically on occasion. Still, regarding the matter of touch, they can be more sensitive to development. They might be more ready when there is abrupt development close to them, similar to when a ball comes straightforwardly at them, or a person unexpectedly embraces them from behind.

They are loaded up with a surge of adrenaline like they are being assaulted.

They can respond too promptly, fleeing at the smallest development or moving to a guarded position. They don't care for whatever will upset their daily schedule and self-control.

Sounds are a specific worry for these people. They can see sounds and commotions more noticeably than most. Music that is common for us, may as of now be excessively uproarious for them. Certain beats, which might be drawing in and may even nudge us to move, might be excessively rough or hard for their resilience.

Due to these overabundances, they are destined to withdraw from boisterous and unexpected clamors, favoring quiet or soft music. There is a more noteworthy inclination for them to dodge high-traffic regions, parties, live performances, or pressed groups. They might need to go to a general store where there are fewer people. They may live in calm areas or excursion in disconnected strange traveler locations.

The sense of sight is a worry for them. They are more specific regarding the things they see. It could be an eruption to the specific tint of an item, the brilliance or obscurity of a specific shade, or basically the disposition of patterns and shadings on a scene. They are in reality acceptable at creative undertakings as a result of this affectability to subtleties. However, it can be dreary for them to have multi-tangible incitement. Glimmering or strobe lights may tire them without any problem. Conspicuous or neon tones might be excessively hard. They may even really like to rest in grave shaded insides or plain walls so their eyes can rest.

Internal upgrades are additionally unmistakably felt by them. They have a lower capacity to bear pain than most. A squeeze might be somewhat aggravating for some, but agonizing for them. An annoyed stomach may warrant a quick counsel at the trauma center. They effectively counsel for clinical help when they feel debilitated or are in pain. They are especially in contact with how their body feels and will voice out worries at the smallest pain. They rush to perceive if their stomach is killing them, if their head is pulsating, or a protuberance is irritating them. They are acceptable patients since they will look for help at the beginning of the illness.

These outer and interior boosts are amplified in the HSP. They will experience a ton of issues on the grounds that others may not be as sensitive to, and may believe that their interests are too paltry to possibly be paid attention to. Relatively few individuals will comprehend their interests out of obliviousness of what their condition is. Then, they are additionally sincerely associated. They are in contact with their feelings and will show them more conspicuously than most. Indeed, even with little improvements, they can undoubtedly be happy, disheartened, incensed, or terrified. Their ability to feel for others, and circumstances, is amplified as though the pain of others is theirs. They might be too influenced in view of the accounts they hear or films they see. Occasions in their lives may be increased to the point of injury. A grievous occurrence like an accident, affliction, or passing may make them be profoundly scared or discouraged.

They may feel a personal obligation or blame when an antagonistic situation develops.

Their responses to these passionate disturbances may be misrepresented, both in sign and length. In the event that the rest are simply pitiful, they can be crying or hopeless. They are the most intense to screech at thrillers, or they may try not to watch it inside and out. They may feel such a lot of outrage inside them, yet they are more inclined to control themselves, collapsing quietly. What others may feel for minutes or days will become weeks, months, or even a very long time for them. They may hold resentment for an exceptionally prolonged stretch of time, be influenced by a pitiful story for quite a long time, or never recuperate from the demise of a friend or family member. They feel as though these occasions have simply happened as of late, with the subtleties ever new in their psyches. Be that as it may, in one sense, they can be advocates for causes. On the off chance that they feel certain about specific interests and concerns, they will make themselves understood. They will feel enthusiastic about personal issues and rally individuals to help them.

At last, they tend to embrace an internal methodology. They like to consider their own or consider things longer and more completely than others. They might be portrayed as reserved or modest because they would prefer to ponder things all alone. They are more independent, tuning in to their own emotions and blocking out the sensations of others. Rather than looking for help from outside, they will support their sentiments and wrestle with these all alone. They would favor quiet, not on account of the absence of hearable improvements, however, more as a result of the isolation needed for speculation and reflecting.

Once more, these perceptions may not matter to everybody. Not all of them are bashful but rather most would like to draw inwards. Not all of them might be sensitive to light, but rather most may have a specific affectability to a specific tactile incitement. Each of them is unique and extraordinary, communicating their affectability in their specific ways.

What makes individuals become HSP? An investigation by Acevedo, et al. (2018) has zeroed in on a hereditary-based attribute called Sensory Processing Sensitivity, which is more evolved in a Highly Sensitive Person. In this examination, they had the option to outline mind circuit designs among individuals with this condition and contrasted it and the brain hardware of those influenced with Autism Spectrum Disorder, Schizophrenia, and Post-traumatic syndrome. Results show that all these four conditions invigorate the precentral gyrus, a piece of our mind that is associated with cognizant development. Additionally, the caudate, thalamus-cingulate, and default mode network which incorporates the fleeting, parietal, and precise gyrus, were actuated in HSPs. These focuses are answerable for intelligent reasoning, engine, and intellectual control. This anatomical connection may clarify the way that they are all the more internal-looking and self-intelligent, sensitive to their activities and the sensations of others.

However, what distinguishes the tangible handling affectability in them from the other obsessive mental problems is the enactment of mind structures liable for hormonal equilibrium, quiet, sympathy, restraint, and self-intelligent reasoning. This is a significant distinctive factor because they are ordinarily mixed up to have schizophrenia or a chemical imbalance. As opposed to having an inadequate, free memory as in schizophrenia, HSPs, truth be told, have a decent handle of memory. They are ready to incorporate their enthusiastic, psychological furthermore, tactile framework differently to individuals with chemical imbalance who will in general need passionate knowledge. We accentuate here the way that the life systems of the brain of these people direct the sort of conduct they show.

Understanding what implies being a highly sensitive person is urgent in our way to deal with individuals, particularly children, with this personality attribute.

They are not intended to be relieved in the feeling of removing portions of their personality that may appear to be badly designed for us. We need to comprehend that they are typically individuals who have a specific personality that isn't shared by the more noteworthy greater part of individuals. Their very life structures direct their distinction in reasoning, feeling, and carrying on, with the goal that they are slated to be more sensitive than others.

CHAPTER 2:

How to Determine if a Child Is Highly Sensitive

A highly sensitive person (HSP) is one of fifteen to twenty percent of the population with a finely tuned nervous system. An HSP has difficulty filtering out sensory input around them; every noise, smell, touch, action, and movement around them is not just noticed, but also deeply processed.

Imagine you are armed with a video camera in a crowded room, trying to capture everything going on in that room. It's not just difficult if not impossible, keeping track of it all but it is also exhausting. It's a good way to visualize how a highly sensitive mind operates when faced with a lot of sensory input — it's trying to make sense of everything going on around it. The nervous system becomes overloaded with information.

This is why highly sensitive children (and adults too) become easily overwhelmed — they are processing everything around them to such a depth that it exhausts them. The overload manifests itself in meltdowns, tears, aggression, withdrawal, or even screaming. Emotions are unconscious reactions to a situation, and they overtake a child. A child often has no idea why they feel the way they do, and they are certainly not in control of their emotions.

How do you recognize a highly sensitive child? There are common behaviors and traits that parents see in their HSCs, but there is no definitive one-size-fits-all list of characteristics. Elaine Aron has developed a questionnaire that helps you determine if your child is highly sensitive. Note that she also emphasizes that you may see only one highly sensitive associated trait in your child, but that that one trait is so true you can be sure you are parenting an HSC. Other parents see a multitude of behaviors and tendencies that convince them their child is indeed highly sensitive.

Aron explains high sensitivity with DOES:

- D — Depth of processing
- O — Overstimulation
- E — Emotional responsivity/empathy
- S — Sensitive to subtleties

Here are some common examples of highly sensitive behaviors or traits:

- Highly sensitive children do not respond well to change in their environment. If they go to school one morning and they are presented with a new, unknown face in front of their class because their regular teacher is absent, their immediate reaction may be to resist entering the classroom.
- Highly sensitive children have problems with transitions. Moving from one activity to another commonly brings on tantrums and refusals to cooperate. The idea of transitioning from one place to another can cause HSC stress, which outs itself in disruptive behavior.
- An HSC often has difficulty with separation from trusted caregivers.
- HSCs take on the emotions of others; they soak them up like a sponge.
- HSCs feel pain intensely.
- A highly sensitive child often has a strong startle reaction to (unexpected) noise. The sudden onset of a test of the fire alarm can bring on tears and fear, and put a child on edge for

the rest of the morning. Such an incident can create negative associations with a particular place.
- Highly sensitive children like the familiar. The unknown is scary. They like to be able to picture where they are going and what they will be doing, and if they can't, they may dig their heels in about going somewhere.
- HSCs have an affinity to nature and animals.
- Clothes labels, sock seams, scratchy materials, bright lights, constant noise (like the humming of a fridge, for example) may make a highly sensitive child physically and genuinely uncomfortable.
- HSCs often don't tolerate spicy or strongly flavored foods or will reject certain food textures.

Remember that being highly sensitive is not a flaw, disorder, or illness. It is not something you necessarily need to consult your doctor about. High sensitivity is simply a set of characteristics that make up who you are. The younger a child is, the less capable they are of filtering sensory input. If we use the bucket analogy, this means all sensory input ends up in their bucket. Part of parenting an HSC is about designing a toolbox they can use to help them decipher what is important enough to go in their bucket, what they can ignore, and how to empty their bucket when it starts filling.

Preventing a bucket spilling over is, of course, the aim, but it's not always easy.

Building in quiet and calming moments, or opportunities to release (emotional) energy, into an HSC's day is an essential part of the toolbox to prevent an HSC's bucket from spilling over.

Discovering what works for your child is potentially a lengthy learning process; a question of trial and error. Once you discover what helps your child, you can build up a 'bucket emptiers' list to keep on hand to step in when your HSC needs help.

CHAPTER 3:

Prejudices About the Highly Sensitive Child

In recent years, the term "highly sensitive child" has become popularized and is now increasingly utilized in schools. However, there are prejudices about this term that should be addressed to provide a better understanding of what it really means and how it's a positive trait, not something to be ashamed about. This part of the book tackles these prejudices one by one, as well as providing information about how parents can help their children overcome the challenges this trait imposes.

1. "Highly sensitive kids are very bad at rebelling."

This is perhaps one of the most common misconceptions about highly sensitive children and may be the main reason why highly sensitive children are often neglected by their parents. The key to overcoming this misconception is to show respect for your child's feelings and personality, just like any other child. This will grant your kid a sense of belonging in the family and will aid him or her in becoming more independent in the future. However, overly sensitivities can also be a sign that something needs to be fixed. If you think your child is highly reactive, you should seek help from a professional who can diagnose what's wrong with him or her.

2. "Highly sensitive kids are very emotional."

While this is true, it can be explained by the fact that highly sensitive children are extremely empathetic towards others, and thus feel the emotions of those around them strongly. This means they will cry at movies or when watching scenes of animals being hurt, but also can be a positive trait if this sensitivity is directed in a good way and serves as an inspiration to help others. For instance, many great artists, thinkers, writers, and philosophers have said that their sensitivity was one of the main reasons for their success in life.

3. "Highly sensitive children are very thick-skinned."

This may be true, but it also depends on their experiences and how they view sensitive people in the world. On the one hand, the most empathetic person can become a victim of people who see him or her as an easy target. On the other hand, sensitive kids can focus on what's best for others and understand why someone may act so negatively towards them just because they are too empathetic. As a result, highly sensitive children will tend to have very good personalities that help them establish themselves as trustworthy people amongst others.

4. "Highly sensitive children cannot change. They are doomed to be this way."

Highly sensitive kids can change and develop into highly successful people if their parents take the right steps to help them. Highly sensitive children, like any other children, should have a healthy diet that includes fruits and vegetables, but should also have some fun foods such as chocolate or ice cream from time to time. Doing these things will help highly sensitive children keep the balance they need to be successful later in life.

5. "Highly sensitive children always feel intimidated by new situations."

While it is true that being exposed to new situations makes highly sensitive kids very uncomfortable at first, this feeling of being intimidated will go away with time as they get accustomed to a new place. The key to overcoming this is to be patient with your child and see them through the process. This way, your child will not feel so overwhelmed by new situations and will be able to deal with them in a more composed manner.

6. "Highly sensitive children love cameras."

This is incorrect information as many years of research have shown that highly sensitive children do not have a knack for photography, but rather have a natural tendency to become very empathetic towards others in need, and thus tend to become photographers at heart. This means that your child would value images of people's dignity, animals' suffering, or natural beauty more than they would picture of themselves, their friends, or family members.

7. "Highly sensitive children do not have any friends."

Again, this is not true and can be explained by the fact that highly sensitive children need time for themselves in order to relax and come back with renewed energy. They like to befriend others during a certain period of time, but then the need to be alone overtakes them and they lose contact with their friends. This is how highly sensitive children work and there is nothing wrong with it because they are just very different than other kids. They react differently to stimuli, which is something all parents should have in mind when interacting with their child, especially while making new friends for playing around with. However, if you notice that your child doesn't have any friends at all, you should seek help from a professional who can diagnose what's going on with them and find ways to make them feel more comfortable in their new environment.

8. "Highly sensitive children are a lost cause when it comes to sports."

While it is true that highly sensitive children may not have as much stamina as other kids, they are very creative and love exploring. This causes them to thrive when it comes to team games where they don't have to be the leader, but rather take orders from someone else. If your child is sensitive and you want them to participate in a sport, don't force them to do so. Rather, help them find the right sport for their personality in order to make the whole experience much more enjoyable for everyone involved.

9. "My child is shy."

There is no need to conclude this from the fact that your child is highly sensitive. On the contrary, if they feel comfortable around other people, they are probably not shy at all. However, as human beings, we all have different personalities and ways of dealing with anxieties, which means that some children may be more easily embarrassed than others and may also suffer from anxiety disorders related to being overly vigilant of what's going on around them. In these cases, for instance, your child may not feel totally comfortable in a new social environment and may need some time to get used to it.

10. "Highly sensitive children have too much self-control."

Highly sensitive children do not have any more self-control than other children, and in many cases, will lack the self-control needed to handle some situations they encounter. This is because highly sensitive children have difficulty controlling their emotions when provoked and being excessively cautious can make them more frustrated and anxious than others.

If you notice that your child has difficulties handling things they shouldn't or needs more support than others, it is best if you seek help from a therapist who specializes in learning disabilities.

11. "Highly sensitive children are just a phase."

This is one of the most insensitive statements that parents make about highly sensitive children. Not only does it show a lack or lack of experience in raising sensitive children, but it also completely disregards their inner core and will instead force them to adapt to the norm without any remorse.

12. "My child is a loner."

Being a loner is not by definition linked to being highly sensitive. In fact, highly sensitive children can have friends, but they may not need as many as other children or more "typical" ones. In any case, all that really matters is that your child is happy and feels comfortable with the friends they choose to hang out with, and this should not be a problem unless you don't encourage your child to play with others to avoid being called pushy.

13. "I should never tell my child off."

This is a common mistake many parents make and is one of the most common causes of parental alienation. It's also relevant to avoid raising your voice and getting angry, which in turn will result in a decrease in sensitivity and self-control. If you want to reprimand your child, experiment with putting them in their place in a non-confrontational manner. For example, "If you don't clean up after yourself, you won't be able to help me."

If you do end up disciplining them, you must model the behaviors that are expected from your child. This shows them that you're not only talking the talk but walking the walk as well.

14. "I should never ask my child to do too many things at once."

The younger the Highly Sensitive Person is, the more intense their feelings become when they are overwhelmed by too much work of a mental or physical nature. Their sensitivity to all stimuli heightens, and their self-control decreases, which may result in an emotional breakdown or regression like bedwetting or separation anxiety.

It is not that HSCs cannot tolerate a lot of stimulation, but they need time to recoup.

15. "Watch for the moon and let it guide you."

For a highly sensitive child, you need to understand their nature and learn how to honor and respect it. They are highly intuitive beings who can read the moods of others easily. They feel their environment deeply and process it deeply, so they can become easily over-stimulated by the fast-paced world we live in today with all of the noise, stress, media distractions, and expectations from parents and teachers.

They need as much one-on-one time as possible — time just focusing on them with no interruptions from technology or other people. They need more time to do less. And they need a lot of downtime — to just be and feel their own feelings.

16. "Highly sensitive children cannot function in our stressful world."

This is a very common misconception that many people have about highly sensitive children. In fact, highly sensitive children may have trouble dealing with all the stimuli that surround them, but this does not prevent them from being successful in their lives when they are given the proper support and guidance throughout the years.

CHAPTER 4:

How to Explain to Others That the Highly Sensitive Child Is neither Capricious nor Too Shy

Surely you have heard someone say that an HSC is too shy a child or just needs to grow up and learn not to be so timid. This is an understandable misconception, but it's also not the whole story. Allow me to illuminate for you what the difference is between a shy child and one who is highly sensitive.

Many children are born with a heightened sense of empathy, which supports them in problem-solving, understanding how others are feeling, and being more accepting of themselves and others in their lives. This can be both an intrinsic trait, as well as something learned when parents behave empathically towards their children from an early age.

This part of the book does not address what parents can do to help a highly sensitive child, but rather what the highly sensitive child is going through and how you can avoid interfering with their growth. Because the highly sensitive child is born with a more active mirror neuron system, they are more able to read others' body language and facial expressions to assess their position in the social hierarchy and alter their own behavior accordingly. This trait has allowed humans to evolve more quickly as we are now able to predict how others will behave instead of just reacting to them.

The highly sensitive child is more likely to experience negative emotions in response to situations that do not matter much to them, such as bullying, abuse, or neglect. They tend to be more sensitive to others' facial expressions, voices, and gestures for them to assess the social hierarchy and how best they can respond. For example, a parent who hugs their highly sensitive child may put both of them at ease because the child does not feel threatened by the supportive gesture. However, an insensitive hug will lead to a negative response from the child who may end up feeling unsafe in your arms and thus crave affection from other caregivers.

The benefits of being highly sensitive are evident in a child's growth. They tend to grow up to be more compassionate and aware of how they are affecting others, even when they are unaware of how they are feeling and thinking. They also, on average, have a higher empathy quotient which can be measured by placing the child in an emotion-provoking situation and then measuring the amount of time it takes for them to recognize their own emotions instead of looking for others' emotions.

It's important to not only understand that a highly sensitive child is not just shy, but also experiencing a struggle that may take some time before they learn to be more self-assured regarding their feelings and actions. Given the correct upbringing, they have the potential to help others feel safer and more loved.

The highly sensitive child (HSC) is not a new phenomenon, but the reasons for the child's heightened sensitivity are still not well understood. Research suggests that in general, the HSC has a greater neural response to non-threatening stimuli than other children. The presence of the HSC appears to be related to more advanced cognitive functions which allow this individual to recognize and respond appropriately in response to non-threatening stimuli and situations.

The roots of sensitivity

The roots of sensitivity are often found in childhood experiences. Some individuals are born with a slightly more delicate constitution than others, but they can usually become less sensitive as they get older if the traumatic events of childhood are replaced with comfortable experiences. However, children who have experienced difficult times, often develop sensitivity due to the painful emotions they felt at the time. Another possibility is that sensitive children may be born into families where there are many other highly sensitive people (HSers), which makes them more likely to be sensitive themselves and allows them to learn how to manage their emotional needs in ways that others don't understand. These are some of the common experiences that can lead to a highly sensitive child:

– The main caregiver is highly sensitive, which means that he or she cares intensely about everything. He or she has a strong need to be emotionally close to his or her children and wants them to feel loved. However, if the child's needs are too different from the parent's temperament, they may experience an intense amount of frustration and may start to resent the child's very nature.

– The main caregiver is sensitive, but he or she does not know how to raise a sensitive child. This lack of understanding can make both parties feel isolated.

– The main caregiver is not sensitive, but the parents are strongly bonded in other ways. If both parents have a hard time understanding how to raise a sensitive child, they may try to compensate by spending a lot of time with the child and giving him or her more freedom than they should.

– The child has relationships with extraverted peers (and/or siblings) who don't understand the need for peace and quiet. This usually leads to some sort of conflict between the highly sensitive child and his peers, which can result in bullying and hurt feelings.

– The child is overstimulated in an environment that is too noisy, busy or chaotic for him at times.

– The child is constantly asked to do things that he doesn't want to do. He feels sad and lonely most of the time due to a lack of connection with his parents (and siblings).

A number of studies have shown that HSCs with a higher cognitive ability tend to have better memory function following specific exposures than HSCs with a lower cognitive ability. This may explain why highly sensitive children often have better memory for details and events, especially those that were traumatic.

HSCs have a more acute sense of smell, sight, and hearing which they reportedly use to "attune" themselves to the environment they are in. HSCs can often tell when someone is near them when they feel vibrations or hear their voice before actually seeing them. HSCs can also identify different kinds of people after initially meeting them by the scents their body releases.

Highly sensitive children are quick learners and absorb all information around them like a sponge; this includes both positive and negative things. They are quick to sense whether or not someone is trustworthy.

They have a stronger reaction than adults to caffeine, sugar, alcohol, cigarettes, and prescription drugs. They can become dramatically affected by electric or magnetic fields from computer monitors or microwaves. They can also be affected by a change in diet, environment, and even hormonal changes in family members (often attributed to their empathy).

HSCs have a more acute sense of smell than the average person. As such they often dislike certain smells that most people find pleasant such as perfumes used by other people (for example their teachers).

CHAPTER 5:

How to Distinguish Between A Highly Sensitive Child And Real Disorders

Sensory processing sensitivity and high empathy have been linked with HSC. Some people might say that the highly sensitive child is just a kid that is not used to being singled out. They are just a normal child that is identifying and noticing things in life that others are not. It would be said that these kids are kind and sensitive. They can become your best friend, but they could also be your worst enemy.

Scholars have made the distinction between an HSC and someone suffering from disorders based on specific signs and high-strung behaviors. They can be diagnosed by professionals or by parents, but their symptoms will all correlate with each other to make up the disorder.

Many researchers believe that there is a difference between someone highly sensitive from birth versus those who are more sensitive because of trauma or chronic stressors in their life. The difference between the two types of children is their patterns which are different.

Many of these children will be able to disregard their own fears and listen to what others have to say. They can have a very high level of empathy for others and will use this ability to try and help other people in pain. They will take on the feelings of others, sometimes not realizing how they feel about certain things.

They may be overly supportive and caring toward others, but they can also be very hard on themselves. They may worry about way overblown things, but it helps them cope with situations that may be very difficult for them. The highly sensitive child may be over-sensitive to the sound and volume levels of things.

They may also have trouble in school because they are highly sensitive or find it difficult to sit still, listen, and concentrate. This can make them seem restless and they might spend more time than most children thinking about something that has happened.

Someone who is an HSC can take on other people's emotions and feelings, so they can enjoy them. They will be very aware of other people's moods, insecurities, and problems but often do not understand how these things affect their own life or what negative effects they could have on themselves. They might make quick decisions and have a hard time thinking of anything other than the problem that they are facing.

They may blame others because they feel it is the only way to take away their own feelings of guilt, anger, or grief. They can blame others for things that have nothing to do with them and not realize what is happening in their own life. Some HSC's can develop eating disorders or develop behavioral problems such as substance abuse at an early age. Many times, these children are very sensitive to different kinds of things, but the only thing they can think about is how to handle the situation.

The highly sensitive child will often become more hostile when on a diet or lose weight without good reasons. They can become very self-conscious and feel like they are being judged by those around them. They often feel that people are not paying attention to them or making fun of them. Many of these children feel like outsiders and will be bullied by their peers because they stand out from the rest of the crowd. Some consider this as a kind of cruelty, but it could be a way for others to get attention from those around them.

Children who are highly sensitive do not make decisions very easily, even when it comes to getting dressed in the morning. They can take much longer than others who might have more sensitivity than they do but want to get through their routine as quickly as possible so they can spend time with friends or family. They may have short, but intense relationships with others. They can be very cautious when it comes to meeting someone new because they are afraid of being hurt or betrayed by someone they love.

Because of their sensitivity, it is important for parents to understand what is happening to their children. There are many therapists who specialize in children who have certain kinds of disorders and will work with the highly sensitive child on a plan that will make them feel better about themselves, and also help them cope with difficult situations in life. When their needs for sensitivity or empathy are met, they can feel a lot better about themselves and not feel like they are different from anyone else.

Highly sensitive children react differently to food and environments than others. They can be very sensitive to medication or chemicals and are more prone to having allergies. They may also be more prone to toxic reactions when exposed to environmental toxins.

Studies suggest that one-third of highly sensitive children have sensory processing problems, which means they're unable to filter out irrelevant information from the world around them. This results in constant over-stimulation; therefore, these children often get easily over-stimulated in the classroom or other busy places such as shopping malls and supermarkets. There are many things for a highly sensitive child to notice when they are in a roomful of people, or something they did not notice, before will stand out like a sore thumb.

Highly sensitive children tend to pick up on social subtleties that others miss. They are very sensitive to tension in their family or the social situations they are in. They might notice when someone is uncomfortable or upset about something and try to help. This can be a good thing, but at times, it can make them feel like they don't belong with their peers or that they are different. An HSC might lack self-confidence because of this and believe that everyone else is normal and actually better than they are.

It is important for an HSC's parents to provide a safe environment where they can feel protected and understood without being criticized. Parents should be aware of the things that trigger excessive fear in their children and help them learn ways to handle these situations so it doesn't become a bigger issue. Parents should watch for things that may be too much for their child to handle. They should also learn how to decide what is or isn't too intense as far as the people around them are concerned.

Parents of a highly sensitive child can help by putting a lot of emphasis on the positive and helping them understand that they are different, but not in a bad way. They should also watch out for signs of depression, anxiety, and other mood disorders. If these kinds of symptoms are found, parents should get their child help at once because sometimes they can become severe enough to lead to self-harm.

CHAPTER 6:

The Situation in Which Parents Are HSP

Parents of sensitive children are often keenly aware of how the world affects their children. They notice what others don't; they notice when their child is upset or overwhelmed; they notice when other children are struggling to manage their emotions or engage with the world around them. The result can be an intense level of engagement with, and parental sensitivity too, the needs of the child that doesn't stop at home. This type of involvement in a highly sensitive child's life can be far from ideal — both for the parents and for their highly sensitive son or daughter.

The situation is so common that we can call it the Highly Sensitive Child (HSC) situation. The Persecuted Character Syndrome: Parental over-involvement.

"What I perceive as critical is driven by my sensitivity, which often makes me feel like a victim of a hidden world out to get me."

Parents are often highly sensitive because they're highly attuned to their child's needs. It's only natural that most parents prioritize the protection of their children and will do what it takes to make them happy, healthy, and safe. But this can translate into a constant cycle of management and caring for the child that can have detrimental effects.

An HSC's parent is constantly adjusting to his or her child and his or her environment. The HSC's parent is highly attuned to what their child wants, so they go out of their way to provide it. They think ahead and anticipate their child's needs; if they don't know what their son or daughter needs in advance, they're quick to respond when they see a problem brewing.

The HSC's parent is highly attuned to what's going on around their child, so they go out of their way to provide a safe and protected environment. They keep track of where their child is and who he or she is with — making it hard for the HSC to spend time with other children. They keep track of when their child falls behind in his or her schoolwork; they keep track of how much sleep he or she needs, and when he or she needs it; they keep track of who's bullying him or her, how he or she feels about it, and what they're doing about it.

The HSC's parent is highly attuned to how their child feels about them, so they go out of their way to make sure that their child feels loved and needed.

An HSC's parent may be literally over-involved in his or her life; as is often the case with people who care too much and are too sensitive to criticism, the HSC's parent may also be gifted with a highly developed sense of responsibility. If you're naturally responsible, you recognize your children's needs before they do, and then go out of your way to fulfill them.

An example: A mother hugs her young daughter before she goes off with friends for the evening. The daughter pulls away and says, "I don't need a hug, mom." What is the mother to make of this? If she's highly sensitive, she'll interpret it as a sign that her daughter wants to be independent. Her daughter needs to feel independent so that she can develop into a well-adjusted adult who knows how to manage her own responsibilities. So, the mother will insist on hugging her daughter or keep track of where her daughter goes.

If the HSC's parent is highly responsible, however, he or she may take their child's apparent desire for independence as an indication that they're failing somehow — failing their children and their own sense of what's right. This prompts a parent to take action.

HSCs may be endlessly supervised by their parents, which can lead to problems for the children. If HSCs' parents are overly involved with their children's schooling, this can have negative effects. The HSC's schoolwork takes a back seat because the school is more concerned with how they are doing in other areas. This leads to an overly defined self-concept that inhibits the child's ability to adapt, as well as depression and anxiety if they're not given time and space to process things on their own.

The HSC's parents may also be overly involved in their child's extracurricular activities, which can also have negative effects. Organized sports can lead to anxiety for HSCs, who may find themselves unable to perform or express themselves. But being too involved in extracurricular activities can also lead to burnout and a wide range of other physical illnesses.

Parents of the highly sensitive often find it difficult to say no and afraid of how their children will react when they do so. This is because the parents are emotionally invested in the outcome of whatever issue is at stake. They're like Senate candidates who feel obligated to take a position on anything that's on the table, even if they don't like it.

CHAPTER 7:

The Situation in Which Parents Are Not HSP

Parents that are not a highly sensitive person should worry about their children being overly attuned to stimuli given off by things like chemicals and sounds. Children can be quick to talk, and many sounds may startle them. This can make some parents feel that their child is picking up on a lot more information than they might actually be. However, it is usually easy for children who are highly sensitive to get used to the world around them, no matter how many new things they encounter daily. In many cases, these "highly sensitive" kids outgrow this sensitivity as well, so there is little need for concern about this trait in later years.

Parents of highly sensitive children should realize that children need to have time and space to get used to new surroundings. This can include a new home, new school, or other drastic changes. Parents of these kids should take things slowly with the child and allow them plenty of time to get used to their surroundings. While there are going to be some bumps in the road, it is important for parents not to overreact or become overly concerned because things will likely work themselves out with time. Highly sensitive kids usually respond well when they are given plenty of positive feedback on their reactions. Parents may want to consider slowing down things in their house to encourage a sense of calm for both the highly sensitive child and others in the household.

Parents need to realize that highly sensitive children need a lot of encouragement when it comes to personal success. They are usually very concerned with doing well and making sure that they do not fail at anything, including school work, sports, and playtime with friends. Parents may want to consider talking with these kids about their concerns and encouraging them in areas where they struggle so that successes can be celebrated, even when there are some disappointments along the way. This can help build confidence in these kids so that they feel comfortable trying new activities and tasks as they grow older.

Parents of these kids should always work to encourage them to be themselves, even when it goes against social norms. These kids usually will not react well to being forced into situations that do not fit their personalities. Enforcing gender roles and other social norms can backfire with these children, and they may even start doing poorly in school or at home as they try to figure out how to fit into a situation that is uncomfortable for them. Parents can help by starting early on developing interests and encouraging the child in these areas, even when others are uncomfortable or trying to get them to move away from their interests.

For these kids, expressing their feelings can sometimes be an issue. They usually show these emotions not only in subtle ways but in loud and obvious ways as well. This can make it difficult for them to connect and talk about how they are feeling with others. Being a Highly Sensitive Child can give parents a lot of information about what the child is experiencing daily, but it is still important for parents to act as a mentor so that kids do not feel like they have to protect themselves from the information that they may be receiving from their highly sensitive children.

If you are a parent of a Highly Sensitive Child, do not feel that you have to be highly sensitive to communicate with your child. Many of them will pick up easily on more subtle reactions and feelings from their parents, and this can help them to know that they are being cared for. In many cases, these children will actually grow up to become highly sensitive adults themselves.

If you are the parent of a Highly Sensitive Child, consider helping others around you that are having trouble understanding or talking to their kids about things like strong smells or loud noises. You may also want to work with these kids on choosing activities that they enjoy so that they can enjoy the experience even if new things can sometimes be overwhelming.

CHAPTER 8:

How to Be a Capable Parent to a Highly Sensitive Child

Highly Sensitive Children have been depicted to be orchids contrasted with different children who are dandelions. This implies that HSCs flourish just in certain controlled conditions and will shrink when put in brutal spaces.

On the off chance that you push them a lot in going to sports and playing b-ball with their friends when it isn't their advantage, you will just separate them and smash their soul. If you just let them do the things that they need to do, at that point they may get ruined and subject to you, unfit to work at different parts of society without your quality. A decent blend of adoring order, firm direction, and loosened-up tolerance will surely make your child blossom.

Here are a few focuses to consider when you are starting to appreciate and sustain the endowment of an HSC.

Acknowledge Them

The most ideal way you can at any point deal with an HSC is to acknowledge your child unequivocally. Disclose to them that they are wonderful, all around. Embrace them continually and make them feel uncommon. At the point when they feel that they are acknowledged, they will end up being their best selves for you. At the point when you love them unequivocally, they will need to cherish you back and others as well, with a similar receptiveness and regard as you showered them.

It might be fairly evident that, however frequently, acknowledgment isn't the main impulse of a parent with a Highly Sensitive Child. They can be mistaken for the blessing, depleted by their fits, and even disparaging of their contemplations and conclusions. At the point when you start regarding your child as an issue to be addressed, they will stay unsolvable and tricky. Your child will be more monitored with you and won't open up their sentiments to you since they feel compromised. Give them the acknowledgment that you provide for your different children.

In tolerating the blessing, don't compare it and different blessings. On the off chance that you have different children, nothing is more frightening than comparing them with one another. In the event that your more seasoned child dominates in games and the HSC doesn't, don't advise them to be more similar to their more established kin. This correlation game is unjustifiable to everybody and sets principles on your children that they don't need and damages their own development. Your child will bring this into their adult lives, corrupting themselves since they are insufficient for you and won't be sufficient for some other norm. They will acquire this relative conduct and rehash this disfiguring disposition to their own children. Quit contrasting your children.

Tell them that they should simply be a greater amount of themselves. Your children are on the whole unique in relation to one another; however, they may appear to be identical. What ties them together is your unlimited love for every one of them. Thusly, the HSC will figure out how to value their uniqueness and won't be embarrassed about being extraordinary.

Build Up a Routine

Make a schedule you can follow consistently. For instance, you can set wake up an ideal opportunity for 7 AM. Your children ought to make their beds, brush their teeth, and take a shower a short time later—breakfast at 8 and off to class. Get kids at 4 PM, extra time until supper at 7 PM. Wash plates, have a shower, and off to bed. Schedules. You probably won't value the force of schedules, particularly in the event that you have an inconsistent schedule. In any case, schedules are significant to HSCs on the grounds that they give them a feeling of control. The consistency of the morning meal toward the beginning of the day, the confirmation of school, the fixedness of sleep time; all give a feeling of tranquility in a Highly Sensitive Child.

Since they know which exercises will occur on specific occasions, they feel loose and can act naturally. There is even expectation of occasions which makes them energized in the event that they like that movement. They can get ready for tests or difficulties that are standard, so their anxiety is controlled. Schedules make for a decent air and great readiness.

At the point when you upset the everyday practice, they can get bothered and lost.

Shocks in the schedules can be extremely upsetting. The pressure subsides when they locate a recognizable face or occasion. In the event that you miss getting them from school at 4 PM, they will begin freezing. On the off chance that they stay up past the point of no return around evening time, they might be drowsy the next day. If you need to leave abruptly for a work trip, which they don't have the foggiest idea, they can feel truly awkward. Little glitches in the routine may encourage some feeling of strength as HSCs are compelled to manage the circumstance. However, drawn-out unconventionality can cause them extreme pressure, and they will be unable to adapt sufficiently. Schedules at that point are extremely remedial for them.

Support Their Interests and Talents

They are quite possibly the most imaginative and skilled of personality attributes.

Due to their meticulousness, the manner in which tones are blended, the structure of pictures, and the movement of notes, HSCs are regular specialists.

Urge them to investigate their gifts by selecting them in workshops, getting them workmanship apparatuses and creates, carrying them to historical centers. Children are at an age where they need steady incitement. The brain is still exceptionally plastic and will grow just to the degree that it is utilized.

Thus, great openness to expressions of the human experience may open imaginative channels for your child. They may not display great imaginativeness from the beginning, yet by simple openness, they may develop into the innovative cycle. Energize your child in the event that he needs to play an instrument, compose a short story, take great pictures, or fiddle with garments making. It is energizing to really focus on an HSC in light of the fact that a virtuoso may simply be before you.

Not all of them, obviously, will flourish in expressions of the human experience. Interests in HSCs can be pretty much as fluctuated as sports, math, and sciences; divider climbing, designing, skating, or PC programming. Every child will be different than the other; however, support them all the same. You or your child may start the investigation of a premium.

The more that you uncover your child, the more data the individual has of what the person in question is acceptable at or needs. On the off chance that your child has a strong issue with a specific action, don't push them too hard. You may need your child to flourish in a specific field; however, in the event that that isn't what he needs, he will do inadequately in it. As parents, we can just help our kids in investigating their own interests. Be that as it may, we can't make them enthusiastic about something by constraining them on it. Allow them to find who they truly are on their own guided by our caring help.

Regard Their Personal Space

In the event that you have shown them the estimation of limits in house rules, likewise, be aware of the children's own personal space. As thoughtful individuals as they are, they will be extremely regional with regard to their space, regardless of whether physical or passionate. The personal space gives them a feeling of smoothness and harmony since it is where they won't be teased for acting naturally. This is a space where they can consider their sentiments to their fullest degree. You might be extremely worried about their opinions and feelings. However, you need to give your children space where they can act naturally without your prying. Indeed, there is open correspondence in the family. However, there ought to be spaces for private contemplations and emotions. You might be welcome to this inward space, but you can't drive your child to disclose the entirety of their insider facts.

Regarding personal space includes shielding a protected separation from the regular space to your child's place. Try not to peruse your children's journals since that is theirs. Try not to snoop on their discussion or tail them at school to check whether they have partners you trust. Quit being helicopter parents, continually sneaking around at your kids. They will disclose to you when they feel that they can trust you, not when they are taken steps frankly. Trust isn't something you request from your children, yet rather, something you procure, regardless of whether they are simply children.

Include the Whole Family

Except if you are a performance parent, the delight and weight of bringing up a Highly Sensitive Child don't rely upon you alone. There is incredible happiness in sharing the difficulties and virtuoso of HSC with others. As a couple, it isn't just the mother who has the assignment to deal with the child. Both mother and father are similarly liable for restraining their children just as appreciating their conversation. You or your life partner might be working. Yet, you ought to figure out how to balance your work with dealing with a Highly Sensitive Child because the demand for attention might be higher in them compared with most kids. At the point when Highly Sensitive Children are pitching fits and you feel excessively depleted to the point of shouting at the child, stop yourself and let the other partner dominate. At the point when you are too occupied to even think about going to class exercises, include your other half so the child actually feels taken care of. This sensitive blossom possibly develops when the two parents are there to cause him to feel cherished.

The elements of kin are additionally a factor in bringing up a Highly Sensitive Child. On the off chance that your child is lonely, they may tend to be caught up in their internal world and manage others during school. Be that as it may, when they have different kin, they should communicate with them, changing themselves to one another's behaviors and personalities, getting into battles, and partaking in games together. Include your different children when you are dealing with an HSC. It isn't such a lot of concentrating about to start dismissing different children. You simply need to make different children mindful of their kin's specific necessities and to be more aware of them. The HSC is a blessing to everybody since they can take advantage of the feelings of the family and tie them together. At the point when a family works in concordance to take care of a Highly Sensitive Child, they are carried nearer to one another and turn out to be more sensitive themselves.

CHAPTER 9:

Developing the Parenting Skills Needed to Help an HSC Grow Up

At this point, you may have some idea of how to take care of your highly sensitive child. They are challenging to take care of, but the rewards far outweigh the stress. When you see your child thriving in school or confiding secrets with you, there is a sense that you have done something right in raising your kids. Celebrate those moments because these are times when you become affirmed of your calling to become parents. Seeing them grow is like harvesting the fruits and enjoying a well-earned bounty.

But your highly sensitive child will not always be a child. They will grow into their own persons, choosing their own careers, picking their own partners, starting their own families, and living their own lives. As parents, you can only be there to support them when this happens. Our duties as parents never end but only change from an active to a supportive kind of parenting. We are partly responsible for their adulthood because the way we take care of them as children determines the kind of people they will become. But HSCs, in general, will have specific challenges in adulthood they will encounter. By knowing these challenges, you can anticipate what kind of preparations you can do so they will be equipped to conquer these challenges.

Becoming Independent Adults

The issue of self-dependence is very real to adults with HSCs. Two extremes in parenting may develop two extreme forms of attachment in adult HSCs. If the parenting type is very cold and distant, where the parents are hard on discipline and cannot tolerate the tantrums of a highly sensitive child, then the adult HSC may become as cold and distant. They will have difficulty opening up to other people because their own experiences of family and parents have not been enriching. They will grow up mistrustful of other people with low self-esteem because they have been subjected to much criticism since they were kids. Some, of course, are able to resist this pattern, but only with much effort. The destructiveness of a cold parenting style will traumatize the HSC until adulthood.

On the other hand, if the parenting style is more of spoiling the child, giving them whatever they want all of the time, then no discipline is learned. Adult HSCs will become very dependent on their parents who have become their sources of consolation and safety. When they feel stressed, their parents will solve problems for them. When they want luxury, their parents will provide for them. When they need something, their parents will be at hand. When the parents are less able to provide, the adult HSC will be mortified that he or she has to face life on his own. The adjustment to adulthood is difficult because they are used to being provided and cared for. It will take some time before they can establish themselves outside of their parents' identities.

The sweet spot is knowing the balance between disciplined parenting and a loving one, making it a disciplined loving parenting style. In this kind of setup, parents raise their children with a lot of unconditional love, providing for them in the measure that they can. But there is also a premium for discipline, where children are given boundaries and made to realize consequences for their actions. With a disciplined loving parenting style, parents will raise responsible adults who are independent and trusting of other people. They will know how to be intimate with other people, but they will recognize boundaries. They will replicate the kind of parenting you gave them to their own children. So, there is a big burden to really discipline and love your kids at the same time.

Establishing Intimate and Professional Relationships

We can never escape relating with others as we grow old. The family and school already set up this socialization process. When individuals transition to adulthood, the interaction evolves to include professional relationships and even intimate ones. After school, your children will have to take up jobs whether as employees, entrepreneurs, doctors, lawyers, or whoever they want to be. But those areas will still involve a lot of interaction with other people. As professionals, HSCs can bring a lot of connectedness in groups. They will do well in creative positions, art professions, or those that involve artistic expressions such as advertising. With their emotional insight, they will do well as counselors, psychiatrists, and medical professionals. They may not thrive too well in professions that are too technical and lack a lot of emotional connectedness. In terms of blending with other people, HSCs must be able to give a good sense of themselves, a solid grasp of their identity. They must be aware of what they want, what conditions will trigger their stress, what kind of work they can tolerate, which personalities they can gel with. With a good sense of self, the adult HSC may establish himself as different from others yet comfortable with it. If the HSC fails to become self-aware, then he will always try to adjust himself to what others want him to be. This can be a tiring process of trying to fit in which will cause a lot of stress.

In terms of workload, HSCs must guard themselves in terms of stress management. They have a tendency to overwork themselves, and this can cause burnout. If you mix persona, family, and professional problems, then they can burst and simply shoot off. In order to prevent this burnout, HSCs must be self-aware as to their limits and how to cope with stress once they feel overburdened. They will naturally retreat to themselves and this is their way of recharging energy. They may not be the ones who like to party away to unload stress, but would rather have a quiet dinner and a good sleep to get ready for the next day. Stress management is needed for HSCs to thrive in the workplace.

Intimate relationships are also a concern for HSCs. They can rather be good at it because they have a good sense of the emotional connection with another person. They may fall in love easily and wear their hearts on their sleeves. But they can also be fooled easily when people take advantage of them. These rollercoasters of feelings can be exhausting for them, and they may think twice when entering new relationships. People who have dated HSCs say that they are thoughtful and sensitive on the one hand but may also be demanding for others. Once an HSC finds a suitable partner, their energy goes into dedicating themselves to their partners and to the family they will form. They will always be the more emotional ones, whether that is good or bad at the moment. Through a lot of experiences, they may learn how to channel that emotional intuitiveness to optimal use in intimate relationships.

Encourage them to explore the world around them

Parents should also be aware that highly sensitive kids usually want to explore the world around them. This is something that they should encourage, but still try to limit any harmful exposures at the same time. A good example of this could be a child who becomes overly excited when they are riding in a car or on a bus. The parent should try to keep them from reaching out and grabbing onto things because it is likely that the child will become easily startled if they are touched unexpectedly while doing this type of exploration.

Sometimes highly sensitive kids can become frustrated if they are not allowed to explore these things independently. This can happen when parents feel like too much of their time is being taken up by their child due to this exploration. It is the parents' job to limit their needs while still allowing them plenty of opportunity to explore the world around them. Parents need to make sure that they are not becoming overly protective of their child because it is likely that they will become frustrated and unhappy with this. The children's sensitivity should never be used as a reason for parents not wanting to experience new things together.

In order to help children overcome their problems with fear, anxiety and depression, they need an environment free from overstimulation. This would include things such as overly bright lights, loud noises, strong odors and excessive crowds. These things can produce too much stimulation for highly sensitive children, some of whom might become very anxious or panic if they are exposed to those types of environments for long periods of time.

Mental Illness and HSC

The strong inner world of the HSC makes them susceptible to a lot of mental illnesses. They get stressed easily and maybe fragile in terms of receiving negative feedback. All of these stressors could easily pile up in their unconscious, multiplying by the minute in their mind. When they have reached their limit in repressing all these negative emotions, they become very vulnerable to several mental illnesses manifesting in their teenage years down to their adult lives. Because they are very secretive in nature, they may be prone to depression as they would want to keep their issues to themselves. For fear of offending other people, HSCs would simply mope over their frustrations on their own. This cycle of thinking negatively about the world, of others, and themselves become a loop in their minds. Without intervention, they can easily succumb to depression.

Since they are also very emotional, significant negative milestones can deeply affect HSCs. Deaths in the family, sickness, unfortunate events, and rejections may be so ingrained in them, they will have a hard time moving on. Their current activities may be hampered because of a trauma in the past. This leads them to be susceptible to post-traumatic stress disorder. Small triggers about the traumatic event can already set them in an exaggerated behavior, which is often self-destructive. As adults, HSCs need to toughen themselves and watch out that their emotions don't control them and their social functioning.

Anxiety will always be marked in HSC. This stems from their bullied past, where they had to go to school and confront all those bullies.

They simply graduate from school but in their adulthood, bullies and the bullied still exist. HSCs still take on the role of the bullied and the anxiety that comes with it. They fear being judged, anticipate negative events, and always think about a grim future; the HSC may succumb to generalized anxiety disorder. Through reasoning out and proper relaxation techniques such as returning to their routine, HSCs can cope with these life stressors and lessen the anxiety they work themselves up on their own.

It does not mean that being an HSC will make you mentally ill. There are a lot of HSCs who can cope well with stressors and live integrated lives. What I am saying is that given the nature of HSCs, they have a higher chance of acquiring these mental illnesses compared to the general population. HSCs must begin by understanding what ails or stresses them and find ways to cope in a healthy, life-giving way.

CHAPTER 10:

Secrets to Raising a Happy HSC

In her book, "The Highly Sensitive Child," Dr. Aron writes: "A Highly Sensitive Child has a nervous system that is finely tuned, aware, and responsive to subtleties. These children become easily overstimulated. They tend to have thin skin and are more affected by outside events than less sensitive children. They are born that way, and it is not a bad or undesirable trait."

Highly Sensitive Children can be identified by the following:

1. They are much attuned to subtle stimuli. This makes them very observant and aware of their surroundings, being able to quickly spot changes in people's moods or expressions.
2. Because they are so attuned to subtle stimuli, they process everything around them thoroughly and deeply. This leads them to have a lot of strong emotions about even the smallest things. If something doesn't go their way, it can make them feel like the whole world is coming to an end!
3. They are very conscientious. This means that they care deeply about doing a good job and making sure that everything is done right.
4. They are highly intuitive, often knowing when something is wrong before anyone else does.
5. They are easily overstimulated by bright lights, loud noises, coarse textures, and busy environments. They do not like to be touched and will push away anyone who tries to hug them or pick them up.
6. They need a lot of downtime, being content to play by themselves for hours at a time.

7. Many are very shy, but this does not mean that they don't also crave attention and love from their parents and caregivers. Even though they may quietly withdraw when overwhelmed, they still deeply desire love and connection with others.
8. They are very concerned about pleasing others and avoiding conflict or criticism of any kind. This is why so many of them become perfectionists early on in life — getting good grades, cleaning their rooms without being asked, etc.
9. They are usually very empathic. This means that they will feel the emotions of others and can become easily stressed when in large crowds or in environments with a lot of conflicts. The best way to describe this is if you have ever been around someone who is crying, you start to cry too; or, if you are around a very happy person, you feel happy too. They may seem this way because they are so easy to read and understand other people.
10. They are usually aesthetically sensitive, which means that they enjoy beauty and art much more than other children their own age. A Highly Sensitive Child may insist on wearing only certain colors or may see something as beautiful that others don't notice at all.
11. They are usually quiet, reserved, and thoughtful, yet they can also be very anxious. They think things through deeply and carefully, but because of this, they get easily overwhelmed by their feelings and thoughts. This is why it is easier for them to spend more time alone than out with other people where they might feel rushed or pressured into doing things they are not ready for yet.
12. Physically, many are very thin-skinned and notice noise or pain more than other children do.
13. They are very conscientious and try to do things right when given the chance. These children usually end up being "good" children despite their difficulties in certain situations; however, this is not because they are "good kids" but because they are sensitive. This means that they will make it a point to behave well when they know that you are paying attention or when their safety is at risk. However, if you aren't watching or if they aren't in any danger,

they may be the first to misbehave just so they can get some attention on them instead of only on everyone else around them.

In the book The Explosive Child, Dr. Ross Greene describes Highly Sensitive Children as "sensitive to sensory stimulation, as well as psychologically and emotionally reactive to events." They are also "driven by a need for exquisite levels of comfort and safety. They thrive in calm, orderly environments with vigilant limits on stimulation."

In his workbook for parents of challenging children, Dr. Greene writes: "They are not the same thing as an emotionally reactive child. The Highly Sensitive Child is physiologically hypersensitive — more easily inflamed by events than most kids are. A Highly Sensitive Child is exquisitely responsive to the people, things, and events in his or her world."

An educational psychologist reports that Highly Sensitive Children are also "more aware of subtle differences in the texture of clothing, or between the feel of different types of paper... they are also more sensitive to unusual odors."

Ruth Elaine Joy, an internationally known expert on giftedness and as one of the world's foremost experts on giftedness in children, writes the following about them: "These kids are often overstimulated by situations that would not bother other kids. They have a low threshold for stimulation. A loud noise or bright light can cause them to shut down. Sometimes they react with emotional outpourings or physical symptoms — nausea, headache, stomachache."

The same author further explains "This kind of sensitivity is not an emotional disorder. Instead, it represents a different way of learning that makes these children more aware, more observant, and more embodied."

Irving E. Sprout and his colleague Janet Sprout-Keck called them "highly reactive children" in their book, "The Highly Reactive Child Syndrome (HRS)." Janet Sprout-Keck was a pioneer in the early 1980s in identifying giftedness as it relates to highly reactive children. In her work, she found that many of the parents of highly reactive children were themselves gifted. This would indicate that they are often a subgroup within the gifted population.

Alice Miller identifies this type of child as "spiritual giftedness — children who can cope with the internal conflicts of life earlier than others."

Highly Sensitive Children also have a greater need for personal space than other children. The typical child needs more space between him/her and all other people, animals, and even inanimate objects. They really dislike it when people touch them or invade their space; they often show disdain when people get too close to them.

It is not only an issue with physical proximity but also psychological proximity that the children will react negatively toward. They are extremely uncomfortable when people psychologically intrude upon them. These children have a more acute sense of space and privacy. They prefer to think their own thoughts without the interference of others.

They can become overwhelmed very quickly by a large group of settings such as birthday parties. They are easily distracted and overstimulated by birthday cake, balloons, games, and friends talking to them all at the same time.

Ellen Notbohm found that Highly Sensitive Children, who grow up with supportive parents, become very hard workers because they want to feel good, avoiding tasks that they know will cause them discomforts such as public speaking.

Sensitive to Light and Sounds

These children are often sensitive to light and sound. Like nature, they dislike abrupt changes in lighting, even using black-out curtains in their rooms to avoid the sun's rays in the morning. As for loud noises, these can be extremely uncomfortable for this child and leave them feeling stressed out or anxious. It is suggested that parents have a special area within their homes where the children can retreat when they need alone time and relaxation because of this sensitivity to their surroundings.

They can also become easily upset by certain clothes or toys. They may not like the feel, sight, or smell of certain items or clothing types which may set off their sensitivities. It is important for parents to be aware of this and to accommodate their child in these areas as well.

Highly Sensitive Children can be identified by their desire for alone time. They will do much better playing by themselves or with one or two other children than in a larger group, as they get overwhelmed quickly when bombarded with stimuli from others.

They also enjoy activities where they can focus on one thing without interruption, such as playing video games, drawing, reading a book, etc.

These children tend to become very intense and focused when doing things that they like. They have an intensity that others sometimes find surprising, especially if the projected image of them is more relaxed and calm-natured. This intensity can be found in both their play and work activities such as musical instruments or math problems.

Many of them can quickly become overwhelmed when asked to do things in a group, such as at school. They may take longer to get started in their seats and begin working if there is too much going on around them. It is best for them if they can work alone or with one child at a time without interruption because it helps to lessen the number of stimuli that they feel bombarded with at any given time.

They tend to be very conscientious and good students. They are very aware of how their grades will make others perceive them, so they usually try hard to get good grades, even if the subject matter doesn't interest them all that much. They are also more likely to be perfectionists or highly detail-oriented in their work.

Highly Sensitive Children can have more difficulty in school because they may have a great deal of trouble going to the bathroom during class. They might need a note from home to use the restroom at any time, and sometimes this requires that they walk by other classrooms where there may be many distractions for them and slow them down. This is especially true if they are often asked by the teacher to check on other students, use the bathroom monitor, etc. It might help if schools were aware of this need and accommodated for it; this would help these children feel more comfortable with school overall and improve their ability to succeed within it.

Parenting these children can be a challenge at times because parents might not fully understand the need for additional accommodations. However, if they are willing to make allowances in these areas, they will find that their child's overall happiness and socialization are enhanced as a result of them understanding why sometimes the demands are placed on them in this manner.

CHAPTER 11:

The Joy of Raising an HSC

The joy of raising a highly sensitive child is often underestimated. They are usually observant, intuitive, and very aware of the outside world. Highly sensitive children are sometimes misunderstood because they don't share their feelings easily or make friends as quickly as other kids. However, when parents realize the secrets behind their delicate qualities and care for them in ways that respect those differences, they may find out that these children offer extraordinary strengths to their families. Children who have a sensitive temperament seem to be born with certain traits. Some of their qualities include:

- They are easily overwhelmed by too much information or stimulation, and they need time to adjust to find comfort.

- They are acutely aware of others' thoughts and feelings.

- They care deeply about fairness and justice, often becoming upset when others do not treat each other kindly.

- They have difficulty when transitions are made, such as starting a new daycare or school and may cry more than others when this happens.

- When they see someone else suffering, they want to make it go away as soon as possible, even if they themselves have not been hurt in any way whatsoever.

- When they get hurt, they want to be nurtured and comforted so that they don't feel alone.

- Their sense of time is very different from most children their age. They may have a hard time understanding the past or future, but they often have a very clear present moment awareness, which makes them aware of everything going on around them.

- If you are an introverted parent who is not used to the constant stimulation and demands of being a child's friend, then it can be overwhelming for your child. You may want to take advantage of his sensitive nature by modeling ways to calm him down through activities that keep his focus on you in all situations. Encourage him to pull you into attention and give you the time you need to read, daydream, or do other activities. He may not know that being with you relieves his stress.

- Educate your child on the importance of self-care. Help him learn about his own physical feelings and capacity to care for himself (e.g., through play therapy, aromatherapy, and massage). Show him how the world can be a safe place for him through things like fun games with siblings and parents, or showing a video by a child psychiatrist who specializes in teaching children how to manage their emotions when they are exposed to traumatic events without isolating themselves from others. In the end, you will discover that raising a sensitive child is both a blessing and a challenge. But if you can identify and embrace his qualities, with patience and compassion, he will learn how to navigate his world and become a more self-confident adult who can care for himself.

CHAPTER 12:

Tips and Rules for Parents of Highly Sensitive Children

Highly sensitive children have trouble coping with their emotions, but by following certain recommendations, parents can help the child cope. A lot of patience from parents is required because highly sensitive children are often moody and easily excitable. Let's consider how to handle a highly sensitive child.

Accept the emotional sensitivity of the child.

Do not try to change the nature of the child. Consider his temperament. Try to find strengths in your child's character.

Give Your Child Enough Time to Calm Down and Cope with Their Feelings

Large crowds of people can oppress him. Therefore, in some instances, it may take him some time to relax and return to a calm emotional state. Do not force your child to participate in group games and activities if he does not like it. Invite your child to do things that calm him: read a book, draw, or listen to calm music.

Set Certain Restrictions for the Child

If you fully accept the behavior of the child, he will not want to change himself. Teach the child to be responsible for his behavior, setting limits for him, and teach him how to interact with the real world.

Encourage Your Child's Efforts

Highly sensitive children may be shy and unsure of themselves. Therefore, praise the child every time he manages to cope with his emotions. Let your child know that you appreciate his commendable efforts. Your praise motivates the child to behave well in the future and increase his self-confidence.

Give Your Child a Sense of Security and Motivate Him

Such children should be rewarded for achievements in school, sports, or any other field. It increases his mood and causes positive emotions.

Develop Your Child's Problem-Solving Skills

Developing your child's problem-solving skills will be beneficial for him in the future. Highly sensitive children experience strong negative emotions because of life problems, so they should be taught to deal with current issues effectively.

Develop Your Child's Communication Skills

Highly sensitive children often experience communication problems and do not know how to express their feelings. Therefore, parents should teach the child to express their emotions and opinions.

Try to Instill Your Child Responsibility for His Decisions

Often, highly sensitive children are overly dependent on their parents. However, the child should be taught to take responsibility for their decisions. The child needs to become independent and self-confident.

Get Your Child Ready for Change

When the family plans for changes in everyday life (vacation, repairs, moving), warn the child and tell him what will happen step by step and what you will do. Include a list of what he should take with him in a suitcase, for example.

Set Time Limits

Even if it is just a change of activity, for example, stopping the game; this change should not be a surprise for the child. Before tearing him away from playing to sit down for lunch, warn him: "In five minutes, we are going to have lunch." The daily routine is also a way to establish a time frame.

Help Your Child Choose From Several Options

If the child needs to choose something, do not offer him more than two or three options; otherwise, he will be confused, may begin to cry, or be capricious.

Do Not Leave the Child for Long

The child's attachment to the parent is actively formed before the age of 9 months. And if mom gives healthy contact, the assurance that "I am here, I am close, I am with you," bodily confirms this, hugging and often picking up, a healthy attachment is formed. Starting from 9 months, you can leave the baby, but not for long. At this age, children can regard the sudden disappearance of their mother as severe stress and loss.

Give the Child as Much Bodily Contact as Possible

All children need to be hugged and kissed a lot, especially highly sensitive ones. When he gets enough hugs, he will get up from your hands and run away to play. But the parent should always be ready to give him this bodily contact.

Do Not Overwhelm Their "No!"

The conscious child's "no" appears at the age of 2-3 years, and it should not be suppressed. If you suppress these impulses, when the child is a teenager, he will not be able to say no to drugs or alcohol, or bad company. He will not be able to say "no" when he will be asked for money in adulthood, etc. He can no longer refuse since his "no" was once suppressed. Do not impose your point of view on the child, in any case, so as not to break his will. On the contrary, try to maintain your child's individuality, his essence.

A Highly Sensitive Child Needs to Be Protected

Highly sensitive children are so vulnerable that people sometimes do not even imagine this vulnerability. They need special handling; you should be more gentle and patient than with others. If an active child can declare himself, draw attention to himself, then these children are so unprotected that there is a danger for them to get psychological trauma. For example, warn and give tips to teachers or people who are in contact with children that he can be afraid of noisy children or the loud voices of teachers. For highly sensitive children, it is traumatic if you do not support them.

Do Not Criticize or Compare with Other Children

For example, you see other children are swimming, but your highly sensitive child is scared. It is necessary to understand that the fear inside him is real so that it is impossible to imagine anything worse. In no case should you say to the child: "Do not be afraid," "You behave like a baby," or "See how other children are swimming." Making any of those comments can only violate the highly sensitive child's self-esteem.

Create a Personalized Schedule for Your Child

It will be easier for the child if he has his schedule. Such children feel comfortable within limits. You can bring such a child to kindergarten a little later and take him away from a little earlier. He will feel more comfortable if he does not meet a lot of other children or parents.

Avoid Aggression and Punishment

Speak as softly as possible in a calm voice, explain everything he needs, and answer his questions in as much detail as possible. Look for compromises without breaking the child's will.

Give Your Child Time to Adapt

If a child is going to a new class, start by offering him just a look. Be close by, providing him with support at this time.

Sometimes a Sensitive Child May Need Specialist Help

For such children, methods such as game therapy, fairy-tale therapy, or creativity can be used effectively.

Most importantly, surround your highly sensitive child with care and love. Soon, he will feel at ease and surprise everyone with his skills.

CHAPTER 13:

Strategies to Support and Calm Your Child

Locate a Safe Zone

The absolute first thing you need to do is to decide the protected zone of your child. At the point when your child turns out to be anxious about an unpleasant occasion, they are highly liable to encounter a fit of anxiety. They may turn out to be so overpowered in feelings and fear that they can't think much any longer and will just leave themselves alone immersed in their feelings. Their response can be misrepresented. This can go from basic crying and outbursts, or trouble to move. Yet, best case scenario, actual symptoms may even warrant a visit to the Emergency room. With alarm assaults particularly, there could be feelings of queasiness, spewing, and trouble for relaxing. A straightforward trigger may send your child into a terrified state.

Rather than additionally terrifying, the absolute first thing you need to do is to quiet down your child. At the point when they are freezing, they have less oxygen flowing in their mind and body. You need to help them with breathing further and slower. Cause them to breathe in and breathe out profoundly with the goal that a greater amount of the oxygen streams in and the noxious carbon dioxide be wiped out. You will see that they will quiet down once they get enough oxygen circling.

Then, you need to recognize a protected zone. What is a protected zone? This is a region or a climate where your child feels generally good and calm.

This is completely reliant on your child's inclination. They may have a sense of security in their own room or anyplace inside the house. They may feel that they are protected when you embrace them or when they are holding a specific toy. They may have a sense of security when they have their earphones playing their music. They may have a sense of security when there are no individuals and there is less commotion. Whatever it is, you need to recognize that climate. At the point when they feel focused, you should have the option to get back to that protected zone. You need to eliminate that pressure by getting back to a position of solace. This will help you with building up a pattern to which you can generally get back. Children need to have a sense of safety, so you need to regard that space. Allow them to withdraw to their protected zone when they feel pushed. At the point when they are more settled, that is the point at which you can handle their contemplations and feelings.

Create Routines and Later Expand Them

Socially anxious children are defensive of schedules. They like things that are unsurprising where they understand what will happen more often than not. They have an extraordinary requirement for control, particularly when they feel focused.

They may follow specific schedules at home, a particular time for awakening and sleeping, for suppers and exercises. Their things might be organized in a specific way and they effectively realize when something is absent or set inappropriately. At the point when they can follow their schedules, they feel especially quiet and troubled. Obviously, when that routine is changed even somewhat, at that point they will feel a ton of stress.

All things considered, we can't adhere to schedules thoroughly. Indeed, there are sure examples of conduct we might be OK with. Be that as it may, it can't be followed constantly because of conditions we can't handle. A specific measure of versatility is required. You should have the option to train that versatility to your children in a manner that is fitting and justifiable for them. You need to regard their schedules, and yet, challenge those schedules to help them with creating versatility.

Two parts are required for this technique. In the first place, we have just talked about the protected zone. Children should have the option to return back to their protected zone, so they feel quiet and ensured. On account of schedules, returning to their routine is a wellspring of security for them. Thus, you need to set up their routine and respect that. In the event that they need to get their work done with a certain goal in mind that works for them, respect that. In the event that they need a specific request to your shopping standard, simply oblige that. They need to realize that they can, without much of a stretch, re-visit their daily practice before you represent a test.

Then, when you need to change their daily schedule, the level of progress should not be excessively intense. It should be not quite the same as their daily schedule, however, not drastically abnormal. For instance, your child is agreeable to just eat suppers at home. You saw that elsewhere, they would hush and not touch the food. To change this conduct, you need to acquaint gradual changes with their daily practice. To begin with, eat together inside the house. Your child will have a sense of security with this course of action. Then, have a go at eating outside the principal house yet inside your home. It very well may be on the yard or on a seat close to the entryway.

The child will always have a sense of security since it is as yet close to your home and that they can, without much of a stretch, head inside. Be that as it may, you previously presented them to eat at a better place. Then, you can have a go at eating at a close-by café or a morning meal place. It should be close to your home so they can feel good. Grow the separation from your home at every supper time over weeks. Do it gradually so your child won't see the progressions without question. Inevitably, they will feel good eating at better places. In the event that you change promptly from eating at home to eating out at a restaurant, they may feel anxious and focused that they will not adapt any longer. The following test for you is to help them with eating in a better place without your essence, for instance, at school. For this, simply follow the gradual changes in the daily schedule.

Be Good Models

There are numerous manners by which individuals learn. A few people learn by perusing a manual and applying the ideas after. These individuals like to comprehend everything in their brains first before they can apply what they learn. A few people learn by doing. They might not know how the thing functions, yet they will simply dabble with it and learn on the spot. We as a whole have our own particular manners of learning. Children learn things in an alternative manner. In contrast to adults, they can't understand manuals, or their appendages may not be prepared to deal with things. Babies and small kids learn by demonstrating. Children will take a look at their connection figures and will duplicate whatever they do.

Displaying initial works through the interaction of connection. Newborn children notice their moms first. They get sustenance and milk from them, so they have a sense of safety with their moms. Since they get food and unequivocal love from their moms, they will feel very connected to them.

They have a sense of security around their moms. That connection is then stretched out to their dads and different guardians. Children see that when they cry and, the dad tends to the issue by changing their diapers or taking care of their milk.

At the point when they have a sense of security to that parental figure, they will frame connections. The level of connection is highly reliant on the consistency of the uplifting feedback. At the point when the child cries, the mother or the dad ought to be there to quiet the child down. At the point when they are reliably present, the connection is strong. However, when there are drawn-out occasions when the child is left unattended, the connection will be poor. The child will imagine that the individual in question can rely upon the parents reliably. They will build up a conditional connection, but with a lot of questions.

As they grow up, children will likewise allude back to their connection figures. They view their dad and mom as awesome and will attempt to copy them. At the point when their parents eat, they will eat. On the off chance that they use spoons and forks, they will utilize those as well. On the off chance that they use chopsticks, they will utilize chopsticks.

They will continually seek their parents for approval of their activities. The connection can turn out to be reliant when the children need to continually allude back to their parents for everything. Social anxiety is overstated when they can't shape autonomous decisions for themselves.

Given such a plan, your responsibility is to be a decent model to your children. On the off chance that they see that you are happy with meeting outsiders, they will attempt to feel good around various individuals. On the off chance that you are vigilant and have not many partners, like to remain at home, at that point, they will be very lonely. On the off chance that you like to connect with individuals in the discussion, your child will feel great shouting out. If that you are the sort to be extremely contemplative, your child will be one.

Arrange With Schools

It is significant for you to arrange with the school in regards to the unique necessities of your child. For certain parents, they would prefer to self-teach their own children or send them to uncommon schools. This has its own upsides and downsides. Yet, you can in any case send your child to ordinary schools furnished that you keep up close coordination with the school. You are not requesting that the instructors offer extraordinary courtesies to your child when you facilitate. You need to clarify the conditions of your child so the instructors can measure the sort of learning measure that will be ideal for your child and his partners. The school is the expansion of the home, somewhere else where children can learn. Along these lines, you need to get your educators associated with the childhood of your children.

You need to screen particularly your child's scholastic execution.

The school arrangement can be an exceptionally anxious-filled climate. We have perceived how a few kids will hush when they need to talk before a class. This can influence a lot of how they will charge in the various subjects. They might be superb at the non-verbal pieces of the exercises, however, may do inadequately openly talking. Your objective isn't to prevent the instructors from doing these exercises. There is a valid justification why this is done and this will really benefit your child by building up his talking abilities. Facilitate with the educators so the way toward tutoring isn't as horrendous.

You additionally need to look out for harassment. Socially anxious children are very likely to be harassed in light of the fact that they are unique in relation to their friends.

CHAPTER 14:

Fifteen Strategies for Parenting a Sensitive Child

Being a Highly Sensitive Child can be trying for the two parents and kids. Sensitive children are all the more effectively over-invigorated by their current circumstances and are more influenced by the feelings of others — two characteristics that may have benefits alongside downsides for these kids. Notwithstanding those characteristics that have been connected with HSCs, numerous additionally experience the ill effects of tangible combination issues and the other way around (Caines and DeAngelis, 2008). To exacerbate the situation, parents whose child is highly sensitive find that their affectability can be confused with issues.

As parents of these children, it's critical to perceive what your child's disposition means for how you raise him. You may have to adjust techniques for discipline, arranging exercises, and making time to simply be together. Here are a few different ways you can help your Highly Sensitive Child have a sense of security in a world that may not generally comprehend his necessities.

1. Use Instinct as a Raising Guide

They have sharp mindfulness about their current circumstances. They might have the option to detect what others are feeling dependent on outward appearance or manner of speaking. You can empower this instinctive mindfulness by zeroing in on building up your own insight into your child's conduct and thought designs. Creating further associations with your child will help you know what's "typical" as far as he might be concerned, and what isn't, so you'll see immediately if something doesn't appear to be correct — regardless of whether he can't disclose to you how he's feeling.

2. Focus on the Faculties in Play at Home

These children — particularly young ones — need a ton of consolation and consistent consideration. This comes as warmth, support, and recess openings. A little sure consideration goes far for these kids. They need to have their faculties drawn in, just as their personalities, through exercises like snuggling up on the sofa, perusing or playing outside with Dad. Make certain to incorporate additional bites and more breaks for the jungle gym when your child is young with the goal that he will not pass up promising circumstances he'll miss once he begins school, and there are more requests put on his time.

3. Hold Your Sensitive Child Back from Getting Excessively Eager

It very well might be trying to measure when your child or children are ravenous, so significantly, you make an opportunity to screen them. They can get occupied to rest or too occupied to even consider eating, which can make them neglect to eat for significant stretches of time. They may be more sensitive to contacting their midsections trying to feel full; this implies that they'll regularly say they aren't eager when indeed they are.

4. Hold Your Sensitive Child Back from Getting Excessively Full

Sensitive kids can struggle with feeling full because their stomachs are extremely sensitive and will swell from simply a bit of food. This implies that you should be cautious about the amount you let your child eat at one time and make sure that on the off chance that he needs to nibble during the day, he gets a modest quantity of food.

5. Help Your Sensitive Child Assemble a Strong Self-Appreciation through Play

At the point when they go downhill enough to go to preschool or childcare, they may discover their partners are mean or even domineering jerks. HSCs may be more sensitive to analysis from parents, instructors, and different adults on the off chance that they don't do well in school or don't appear to be serious enough on the games field. This can prompt them to feel like they are disappointments or "imperfect."

6. What's More Through Tasks

To assemble a strong ability to be self-aware, highly sensitive kids need a lot of freedoms to feel that they are adding to their family and that they have something of significant worth to bring to the table and the world. This is particularly significant for small kids who haven't yet acquired the abilities they need for school (like documenting papers or collapsing garments), however, can be significant for more seasoned children who have had achievement in school and sports, yet at the same time appear to be uncertain about themselves.

7. Ensure Your Sensitive Child Feels Cherished by the Words You Say and the Moves You Make

They are mindful of the feelings of others and everything going on around them. They may struggle with dealing with their own feelings on the off chance that they don't feel adored, or in the event that they end up reasoning negative daydreams about themselves or feeling commonly tragic or apprehensive for unknown reasons. It's significant that they comprehend that being a highly sensitive person doesn't imply that they are not deserving of adoration or regard. All things considered, they need to feel that your adoration is theirs always.

8. Allow Your High-Sensitive Child to Have the Opportunity to Themselves and to Re-Energize

Highly Sensitive Children need time alone to have the option to handle their contemplations and sentiments. They need that time particularly when they are exceptionally young and may not realize how to channel their feelings yet. By giving your Highly Sensitive Child a little space, you'll help them construct a characteristic feeling of equilibrium that they can utilize when their reality feels too loud or confused once more.

9. Ensure Your Child Has the Perfect Measure of Incitement at Home and School

They can't deal with consistent incitement for extensive stretches of time. They're regularly more agreeable at home, in spots where they can feel a specific degree of protection and a suspicion that all is well and good. Accordingly, they may not be as inspired by social exercises like gatherings or gathering trips that may some way or another appear to be enjoyable to different kids their age. HSCs additionally need more opportunities to handle data than others, so furnish them with plentiful freedoms for breaks during bunch exercises — particularly when they are young — so they don't feel hurried or constrained.

10. The Perfect Measure of Personal Time

These children likewise need time to rest and re-energize. They may find that they become curiously worn out when there is a ton going on at home or at school. That is on the grounds that their faculties have been over-burden, which can cause them to feel true, inwardly, and intellectually depleted. It might require some investment for them to recuperate from that sort of extreme experience — especially on the off chance that they actually need to draw in with individuals or do different errands after the underlying over-burden has passed. You'll have to furnish your child with enough vacation so he can unwind and get away, if just for a brief timeframe.

11. Show Your Highly Sensitive Child How to Deal with Their Emotions

They need to figure out how to deal with their feelings — particularly when there's a great deal going on around them. In the event that your child feels like he needs to keep his emotions inside, on the grounds that he would not like to be viewed as "frail" or fall into difficulty, almost certainly, he'll snap when under pressure. Show HSCs how to take full breaths so they can deal with their actual sentiments. Urge them to discuss what they're feeling so they don't restrain their feelings. In the event that you have a younger child who can't communicate verbally yet, help him discover approaches to show you in alternate manners what he's feeling altogether for you both to feel comprehended and upheld.

12. Let Your Highly Sensitive Child Realize That It's OK to Have Those Sentiments

Kids who disguise their sentiments may attempt to conceal them — in light of the fact that they feel embarrassed or humiliated about them — which can really aggravate those emotions eventually. So, promise your child that it's human and characteristic to have a wide range of various feelings, regardless of whether they appear to be senseless, strange, alarming, or awkward. It's additionally imperative to tell kids the best way to manage their feelings in sound manners so they don't need to turn to damaging ones like lashing out or pulling out when they're disturbed.

13. Teach Your Highly Sensitive Child How to Affirm Their Rights

They will in general be really compliant kids — they're normally held and pleasant, and they don't care for causing a ripple effect or getting into contentions. Be that as it may, now and then it's significant for them to figure out how to support themselves when they feel like their privileges are being disregarded. So, tell your child the best way to say "No! That is not reasonable!" or "I don't care for that" in a firm yet deferential way so he can communicate healthily.

14. Help Them Set Limits with Their Friends

On the off chance that you notice that your Highly Sensitive Child is by all accounts continually getting into contentions with different kids, or in the event that he regularly gets prodded, pained, or poked, struggle with displaying solid compromise abilities maybe altogether. Talk about ways he can define and uphold limits and clarify why it's significant for him to tell others when they're pressing his catches.

15. Help Them Acknowledge Approval Benevolently

Highly sensitive kids can struggle tolerating praises since they don't feel meriting them... or in light of the fact that the manner in which a person is offering the commendation makes them awkward. Since they can be somewhat self-basic themselves, they may not comprehend why somebody would say something kind regarding them. You can help your child with learning to get praises nimbly by zeroing in on the positive characteristics behind the commendation, so he'll figure out how to have confidence in them and acknowledge them for what they are.

By giving a climate where your Highly Sensitive Child has a sense of security and safety, you'll give him the space he needs to develop into a balanced, cheerful youngster. Alongside showing him how to really focus on himself and deal with his sentiments, you'll show him how significant of a person he is just by acting naturally. You'll likewise guarantee that he keeps on being simply the best form so he can be his best self in your relationship with him.

CHAPTER 15:

What Should Our Approach Be to HSCs?

If we have a highly sensitive child, should we see his or her personality as a gift to celebrate or a curse we need to break? It is very difficult to raise highly sensitive children, especially if we do not have that personality ourselves. It is hard to understand their behavior because it does not fit in with the rest of society, that they will always be viewed as pushovers in schools and reclusive monks despising social relations. Having a highly sensitive child may even lead us to question ourselves, if we did something wrong during the pregnancy, if we raised them too spoiled or too left to themselves, or if we were bad parents.

The key here then is a radical perspective on HSCs, to view them not as a curse but as a gift we should celebrate, discipline, handle, and nurture. A "gift" is a good metaphor to describe HSCs because they should be sources of joy rather than disappointment, anxiety, or even fear. Gifts are blessings meant to make us happy, the kind of happiness that is not fleeting or fake. As parents, we never know what kind of children we will receive and so it is with HSC as gifts. They are not accidents in a pregnancy outcome or a product of poor child discipline at home. They are gifts that parents receive and should be celebrated, as any child that is born. They may have some peculiarities, but it is those peculiarities that make them special.

It may not seem easy for parents to view their highly sensitive children as kids, especially if they become difficult to handle. But they are children nonetheless who just have different triggers and needs. In the course of trying to manage a high-maintenance child, you might overlook the fact that they have certain talents, abilities, and dispositions which are unique to them and will bring you a different kind of joy. The HSC changes the family dynamics, even binding the family together because of their unique capacity to tap into the emotion of people. They are heart people, wearing their emotions on their sleeves. And this is a good jumping point to highlight the special gifts and talents of highly sensitive children. I will now highlight some of the more prominent gifts highly sensitive children possess.

They are Patient and Keen Listeners

It is actually not hard to discipline HSCs. You may be surprised by this because you may think that they are just simply high-maintenance children. On the contrary, HSCs are good listeners and followers. They have great respect for their parents and authority figures and will follow commands to the rule. This comes perhaps from their need to please people and satisfy that need to be seen as doing what is right. They may also be afraid of being punished. Older children who are highly sensitive turned out to be very responsible in taking care of their siblings. Even without your supervision, they will follow what you say. In that sense, they are actually low maintenance because they are easy to discipline.

Their listening ability is also uncanny for children their age. Since they are very particular to sound and emotions, HSCs would pick up all the details of whatever you say to them. If you tell them that you will pick them up at 5 PM, be sure to pick them up at the exact time because they will listen and follow exactly what you said. They are listening not just to what you say, but how you say things and the underlying emotions embedded in each statement. If you tell them, "Honey not now," they will know if you are tired, angry, annoyed, or simply not in the mood by how you say the phrase. They listen to the smallest nuances of things said and unsaid and this is a good trait. They can sense how people are just by listening to them.

They Excel in School

In general, HSCs do well in school. The academic setting is a place where HSCs thrive because their skills are honed in this setting. The school pushes students to be attentive and particular to details, expressive in language, and methodical in logic. These are areas where the HSC does well. School also wants to develop independent learning; hence, students are given a lot of homework or personal activities to test their skills and abilities. HSCs love this because they can be on their own, concentrating on the work and putting much thought into each item. Subjects such as arts, language, reading, and comprehension are fields where they excel because they have good attention to detail. They know how to mix colors and copy images on paper. They are particular to expressions in language and their memory is extensive. But they will also do well in Science and Math. The thought process involved in logic is something HSCs can be known for.

HSCs would encounter challenges to education when it comes to collaborative work and time management. They would prefer to work alone, but the school will often have team-based activities. School also trains children to work with each other, whether in projects or academic papers. And HSCs would have a hard time jelling in with other children because they have a particular way of doing things. They would either hog up all the work or have minimal participation. Their attention to detail is also something that can be tiresome for them. They can be perfectionists, unable to move on until the details are all perfect. And this can be time-consuming. The work is excellent, but it will take a lot of time. HSCs then won't thrive in time-pressured activities and exams because they like to take their time. But in general, HSCs would regard teachers as their allies and will excel in the school setting.

They Have a Sense of How People around Them are Feeling

HSCs will also be very sensitive to your and your family members' feelings. They can pick your emotional thermometer through your words and actions, and even the things you don't say and do. If you had a bad day in the office, they can sense right away and will steer clear from you. If you are generally happy and carefree, they can also sense this and will warm up to you easily. If you need a hug, they can sense that and will hug away all your pains and problems away. HSCs are very endearing children with high emotional intelligence. They can anticipate appropriate behavior based on the feelings projected to them.

HSCs then also make good friends. They can easily navigate the complexities of friendships and feelings. They know when their friends are fighting with each other, when they are developing crushes, or when they have heartbreaks. They are the go-to-person when it comes to complex personal problems because they are can analyze situations and empathize with people very easily. They can dish out advice that is grounded on sound judgment. They are patient listeners, able to sift between the emotions people feel when they tell their stories. With their keen observance of people, they can spot personality flaws and probable causes of problems. People depend on HSCs for advice, making them the best friend you always wanted to have.

They are Quiet

This is actually a rare gem to find among children and a practical gift you can be thankful for. Unlike other children, HSCs are inward-directed and will require a lot of silence. The silence is a space for them to gather their own emotions, listen to their body, and allows to imagine and create their own world. They are good listeners and observers of people because they are silent enough to let their senses work optimally. This does not mean that they are antisocial. They will relate to others and even be talkative at times when asked. They just have a preference for being quiet, and active when needed.

As children, parents appreciate this silence because it creates a calm atmosphere in the house. People can relax because HSCs demand calmness in silence. They may be prone to tantrums and meltdowns, but these are rare occasions and often triggered by a particular concern. But for most of the time, they can be depended on to learn quietly, listen attentively and think independently. If you are not comfortable with silence, then this could be a problem for you. But silence itself is a gift you should explore and even inculcate in your own life as parents. You will do well to learn from your highly sensitive child how to be quiet yourself to be more self-reflective and attuned to your feelings.

They are Very Thoughtful in Creative Ways

Being good listeners and emotionally connected, HSCs are also very thoughtful. They spend a lot of time composing what they want to say and usually, these are emotional statements that are well-thought-out. They can give honest compliments to people they appreciate. They can constructively say negative things because they put effort into not hurting people with words. They will anticipate your needs and please you even before you ask for them. They are the ones who usually write cards on your birthday or occasions such as Christmas, your anniversary, or Mothers' or Fathers' day. When it comes to their siblings, they want to make sure everyone feels good and appreciated. They will go to lengths to buy gifts for their siblings or to encourage them to do well in school.

HSCs are also very creative children. Give them paint and they will draw, a guitar and they will play, singing lessons and they will perform. These creative activities rely so much on attention to detail which they are good at. They love colors and are experimental on how they can make good drawings and patterns. Their inner world is also powerful due to their imagination. This helps them create characters, paintings, and music that is novel and interesting. The punch comes when they use art to channel their feelings. If they feel angry, they may displace this in a canvass. If they are ecstatic, they can burst into song. They are not afraid to show their feelings and talents. When you notice their interest, develop that further because they are going to thrive in that area.

CHAPTER 16:

How Do You Deal with A Sensitive Child?

The facts demonstrate that we should value our Highly Sensitive Children as blessings and praise their gifts and capacities. Yet, these blessings additionally accompany a couple of difficulties. Like some other children, they will have their emotional episodes and personality characteristics. Once more, I underscore that all children will have certain challenges regardless of whether it is in conduct, disposition, mental turn of events, or relational abilities. There is no perfect kid. Dealing with these children will be the same as taking care of a standard youngster who might be sweet at one time and then hollering in another. What we need to feature here are some of the difficulties parents may experience when dealing with an HSC.

Being sensitive individuals, they will give specific troubles that parents ought to be set up to deal with. They can be debilitating to oversee, particularly if you don't comprehend what is causing them to act how they do. You may get disappointed with them, however, by foreseeing their emergencies, you can monitor your energy and assumptions better just as gotten more patient with them.

HSCs are Prone to Tantrums and Meltdowns

Sigmund Freud, the dad of brain science, presented the idea of the id, the inner self, and the super-personality. He guesses that we all have these three parts, affecting our practices. The id is the piece of our cognizance that manages our longings and needs. The id controls our need to look for joy. The super-sense of self is the piece of our cognizance answerable for complying with rules and decrees. It is in direct differentiation to the id, which has no respect for shows. The self-image incorporates the id and the super-personality together, choosing whether we ought to follow our needs or follow what is directly indicated by social guidelines. The three segments all work to impact what sort of decisions we make consistently.

They are a furball of sentiments and feelings. They are so in contact with them that they may have issues communicating what they feel inside. As children, they will have the unadulterated id, the part of our brain that follows the needs without respect for anything. If they feel anything, they will communicate it without being cognizant if their conduct is suitable or not. They may even cause a situation in the open when they get into a fit. It could be hard to quiet down, regardless of the amount you smooth talk or even chasten them. At the point when the id is delivered, they will be exceptionally difficult to control.

What are the typical things that set off HSCs? Each of them will have a unique trigger to them and the situation. They are effortlessly influenced more than different kids since they are so in contact with themselves and with their sentiments. Any basic thing, for example, not getting the toy they need, not being permitted a specific action, battling with their kin, a lost thing they love, a lot of commotion, or some other outrageous tangible experience may trigger a fit of rage. Much the same as normal kids, these children will need to have their own particular manner and struggle to prepare the various feelings they feel when they get dismissed.

HSCs May Be Particular and Picky About Personal Items

They have a specific method of continuing and schedule that they are specific to. They may fix their things with a specific goal in mind. They may have a specific method of eating their food or a specific surface of texture they are OK with. They might be fastidious about how they look, or aware of the brand of things they buy. If you coincidentally read through their private compositions, at that point you will feel a ton of animosity from them. They have a strong feeling of security and ownership, taking great consideration of their things. If you cross their limits, they will fight back as they feel assaulted. They may even struggle to trust in you the next time if you insult their sensibilities in any capacity.

Tutoring May Frequently Be Trying for Highly Sensitive Children

Even though they dominate in scholastics and individual work, the school setting itself may introduce certain troubles for them. They may have a specific method of learning or doing things that the educator will be unable to give.

HSCs Have Difficulty Handling Negative Feedback

As with different children, they will submit botches. They may pass up schoolwork, turn out to be raucous in class, or surpass set computer game occasions. As parents, your job is to teach your children, giving input in a way that is reasonable for them so they can quit doing practices you feel are not suitable. The issue of input is sensitive for HSCs. It isn't because they are fussbudgets who have high confidence and will take it hard if they fail. Or maybe, they are so in contact with their feelings than negative criticism would be taken hard.

You will drive them away if you abruptly burst into a seething message or even a clobber on their behind. They blame you more than anything. These children additionally will, in general, make things personal. At the point when their work is considered a "B+," they may likewise believe that they are "B+" individuals, insufficient for the norms of instructors or of parents. They experience issues isolating their personhood from their work and yield, so an assault on their work is an assault with the rest of their personal effects. You must be cautious then, on giving them input. Think well about your choice of words since they need that criticism regardless of whether it is excruciating.

In any case, you can bundle it in a way that is less culpable to them or will just zero in on the yield or conduct and not their person.

HSCs Are Targets of Bullying

With increased reasonableness, a well-spring of feelings, and identity with subtleties, they are obvious objectives for harassing. We see this particularly in the young, where socialization occurs with different kids. You can't censure different children for not understanding HSCs because they are investigating how they communicate with other people. Be that as it may, these connections may frequently prompt maltreatments since they may not fit into specific factions of children. They can be pained for their idiosyncrasies; for example, how they dress, their fastidiousness on subtleties, or apparently powerless characters.

Some of them really fight back, which actually opens the entryway for serious pain. Children are as yet finding their gifts and capacities and investigating their social abilities. They additionally want to have a place with specific gatherings, however, the school setting jumbles up with their favored request of socialization. You must be extremely cautious regarding noticing for indications of pain in your HSC. They can be loudly manhandled through verbally abusing or reviling. There could be examples of actual maltreatment when youngsters turn crazy. As opposed to trusting in you, they may simply quiet down and brood over their sentiments.

It may benefit us to talk about this domineering jerk harassed relationship and how it can be developed in school. I need to say that no one is brought into the world a harasser or a harassed. It's anything but a hereditary attribute that we give to our children. Most domineering jerks are forceful, however, there are additionally instances of detached forcefulness that are pretty much as guileful as the immediate ones. Pain is achieved by the interaction of socialization, where personality conflict and animosities are tried. Children are generally unique about one another, having various tastes and likes, looks, and beginnings. Thusly, the variety opens the entryway for the craving of certain gatherings to set up a specific standard. This longing is extremely strong in teenagers where they need to have a place with specific gatherings so they can fit in. If people don't find a way into the guidelines set by the gathering, they can be threatened through the pain.

Bullies disdain variety and will want just that their guidelines are the lonely ones to be followed. Bullies believe that they have a restraining infrastructure on the best way to dress and carry, on the most proficient method to mess around, and who will win. It is an issue of force held by individuals who are simply starting to know what their identity is. The HSC, which exemplifies variety, is the characteristic objective of bullies since they don't fit in.

HSCs May Be Secretive

The internal universe of these children is where they feel the safest. It is a climate where they can act naturally without being judged or constrained by others. It is both a reasoning and a passionate space, where they brood over things they learned, or measure emotions that happen to them. You will discover them for the most part quiet or gazing groggily into space as they are caught up in their inward world. From one perspective, this is a decent personality characteristic since it builds up their self-appreciation, mindfulness, and character. By acting naturally intelligent, they can become more acquainted with themselves better and plan out how best to cooperate with others. Be that as it may, then again, the internal world might be a getaway from experiencing others. At the point when they feel undermined, they will pull out to their inward space, reluctant to go up against the stressor and resolve the issue. This is a method for dealing with the stress they have created because they have discovered that by being quiet, they can close out the issues.

This will become neurotic when the HSC experiences issues that they can't settle all alone. Since they are normally attracted to their internal world, they can be cryptic, supporting their own considerations and emotions to themselves. They won't impart to others their contemplations, emotions, and issues since they believe they are judged. On the off chance that they have an issue in school, they will attempt to tackle it all alone. If they have relationship issues, they will mind their own business. If they are having issues with their sex and sexuality, peer pressure issues, or issues with other relatives, they won't open up without any problem. This is troublesome because the current issue doesn't get talked about and isn't tackled right away. But once more, I underscore that all children will have certain challenges regardless of whether it is HSC or not. There is no perfect kid. What we have featured here are just some of the difficulties parents may experience when dealing with an HSC.

CHAPTER 17:

Advice for Parents of Highly Sensitive Children

Since your child was born, you have worried about whether he is too shy, too intense, or too sensitive for his own good. You have fretted that his heightened reactions to all things could hold him back socially and hamper his academic performance, not to mention his emotional health.

Your concerns were well-founded. Research shows that many Highly Sensitive Children are bullied and teased. They report feeling depressed, lonely, and anxious, though not necessarily when adults around them are feeling the same way.

And yet, as more is learned about the trait that makes your child so exasperatingly unique in his response to all things emotional — you know, the trait responsible for his fierce loyalty to family, friends, and pets — research also suggests that your Highly Sensitive Child's heightened reactions can provide him with an array of gifts as well.

As parents, we want our children to be happy, confident, and self-sufficient. But we also want them to be authentic, inquisitive, and open-minded. We hope that they will tap into their creative sides and become lifelong learners.

We want them to make choices that make them happy today and reflect well on them tomorrow. So, how do you help your child avoid the very real pitfalls of being highly sensitive while making sure that he also takes advantage of its many perks?

One thing is for certain: You must understand his sensitivity, allowing him to set his own pace — both developmentally and socially; and listen closely to what he has to say about his experiences in the world.

But it also means accepting that he is likely to have a number of difficult-to-change traits, such as perfectionism, shyness, and difficulty with transitions. In this chapter, I'll discuss these traits and give you some tips for managing them so that they don't impede your child's ability to succeed in school or elsewhere. Highly sensitive children are quick learners and absorb all information around them like a sponge; this includes both positive and negative things.

In this day and age, when the world is much smaller and controlled by parents, your child's ability to sense danger before it occurs is one of his greatest assets — but also his biggest challenge.

If you're not sure if your child is a highly sensitive child or not, it's easy to figure out what they should do: They should be allowed to choose how much stimulation they want in their everyday lives. If they want to be doing less, then let them; and if they're trying to do more, then let them have a go at something new.

One thing that parents of HSCs often do is try to push their kids into doing all sorts of things, but the truth is that children need lots of downtime. It should be a priority to give your child plenty of quiet and calm time every single day. It'll help them to be less anxious, and it'll also help you keep things in balance as well!

While it's true that highly sensitive children need more downtime than other kids, they also need more time for play. Playing is a really important part of how children develop, both mentally and physically. If you want to be able to play with your HSC, then try looking for things that will boost their creativity and imagination. Playing games that involve a lot of pretend, role play, and storytelling will really help them to blossom.

As well as giving your child more time for play, you'll also want to give them more time to focus on their own needs too. It can be difficult for highly sensitive children not to compare themselves with other kids, but it's important they learn how else to handle the world around them. Do they feel like they have too much responsibility? If so, try finding ways for them to focus on what they really want in life, rather than worrying about how other people live their lives.

Unpredictable or Unstable Environments

The problem is that these children are most likely to get into trouble in predictable environments. That's because they pay so much attention to what's going on and attempt to adhere so closely to rules and schedules that when something unexpected happens, it throws them for a loop — and they act out. Your child may have learned not only to pay attention to everything that goes on around him but also how not to react emotionally or aggressively in many of the situations he encounters every day. But when he's suddenly dropped into a chaotic environment with no set schedules or routines, he doesn't have the tools he needs to respond appropriately. They can thrive in unstable environments as long as they have the stability at home that they can rely on. Many HSC are happier with a variety of activities, friends, and schedules — but with a predictable day-to-day routine at home.

Unpredictable Parents

This is a common problem among these children who are exquisitely attuned to the moods of those around them. Many parents of these children will tell you that their child knows when they're feeling stressed or depressed before they do and will act out accordingly — because he's sensitive to his parent's moods.

Even if you're a happy, stable parent, it can be hard to be around an over-active child. As much as you love your son, you need to have a clear sense of your own needs and priorities in order to be a good parent to him.

Protect Them from Bullies

Bullying is not only physically dangerous but also emotionally damaging. If your child is being bullied at school, take him out of the situation immediately and look into other options for getting him the education he needs.

But before you panic, there are a few things you should know. First, only 5% of kids are actually bullied at school. Second, bullying is most common in elementary school and peaks in the middle school years. It subsides entirely by high school.

And third, bullying makes them especially vulnerable to anxiety and depression because they are so attuned to the moods around them. So, if your child does get bullied, look for signs of depression — or even anxiety disorders — and contact your pediatrician or a child psychologist for advice and support.

Boost Their Self-Confidence

If you take away one thing from this book, it should be this: Your child is sensitive, so he needs to be confident and secure in who he is. Because it takes them longer than most to process information, they are more likely to have low self-esteem because of their academic difficulties.

One of the best ways to boost your child's confidence is to give him plenty of praise and encouragement for his efforts, no matter how small or insignificant they may seem. You can also help him by finding activities that allow him to shine, such as sports teams or a music group. And don't forget to praise him for his sensitivity!

Conclusion

10% of all kids are considered highly sensitive, meaning they absorb the emotions and moods of those around them. This might manifest as a constant need to please people, general anxiety, or even physically getting sick from being around too many people.

However, high sensitivity is a gift. These kids have an increased potential for empathy and creativity that can translate into meaningful work in adulthood. There is research that claims high sensitivity could be an evolutionary marker for higher intelligence, which helps children survive.

In general, the highly sensitive child is not popular with teachers and peers. They get along better with animals or imaginary friends. For this reason, they often develop a strong sense of protectiveness and are often seen as being angry or aggressive when this is not the case at all.

In school, they tend to excel in the areas of writing and reading. They also prefer jobs involving creativity over administrative work.

To help your highly sensitive child, focus on encouraging their strengths and managing their weaknesses.

This may include engaging in less structured tasks, allowing them to withdraw from social situations for alone time, or sending them to a school that is more accommodating of what they need.

Even if you don't have a highly sensitive child, it's important to learn about this trait to better understand the people around you. The world needs more empathy and fewer bullies! — especially as human interactions increase each year over the internet and other forms of technology.

Sensitive children need to be taught how to handle their anxiety and not let it get the best of them. They should also learn how to put their feelings into words, which is a big help in forming the social skills that will help them as adults.

And finally, if you have a highly sensitive child, they will tend to take on your emotions. They are easily hurt and experience their entire bodies when they are upset. This means they have an innate ability to feel what you are feeling. So, if you love them, show them.

THE HIGHLY SENSITIVE CHILD FROM CHILDHOOD TO ADOLESCENCE

A Comprehensive Guide Addressing The Needs Of Specific Age Groups Birth to Age 20

Laura Henry x **Royal Owl Books**

Introduction

Highly sensitive children are easily overstimulated by too much contact, too much noise, too many people in one place, or the wrong kinds of touch. They tend to withdraw from busy environments and crave downtime. This sensitivity may be genetic or learned. Either way, parents must understand and provide a conducive environment for these kids. While they don't need an exclusive setup, certain accommodations will make life easier for them.

Sensitive children have several traits that make their behavior different from that of other kids. Some of these traits are positive, while others can create problems. An understanding of these qualities is key to helping your child thrive.

As early as birth, sensitive children react more strongly than others. They cry when other babies are calm and appear "easier" to soothe. They prefer gentle music or even silence over loud sounds or chaotic playgroups. As they grow, they tend to dislike physical activities like roughhousing and can become upset easily if the game isn't fun for them. The younger years often present many problems for parents with sensitive kids because the behaviors associated with this trait go against cultural norms and expectations—from crying in the church to wanting alone time after a big family event.

The sensitivity associated with this trait can be hard to accept, even for parents who understand that the behavior is a positive one. Many of these kids are often seen as aloof and unhappy. Yet, in fact, they may be quite happy once you learn how to interact with them properly.

In addition to those already mentioned, there are three other traits of highly sensitive children that must be accepted by parents: they have high pain tolerance (they don't complain about injuries and keep going), high guilt tolerance (they don't take responsibility for being scolded or yelled at for making mistakes), and very good emotional recall (they remember things from the past very clearly).

The issue of guilt can be especially problematic in highly emotional children. Even a little misplaced guilt can cause them to shut down and withdraw when they could be learning from the experience and moving on to new things. You may need to repeat a lesson or reprimand your child several times before he or she actually understands it and gets over the guilt.

A parent's attitude toward these traits is the most important aspect of raising sensitive children. Parents who embrace their kids' unique personalities and recognize their well-being is more important than their behavior, will have an easier time raising highly-sensitive kids. The more you anticipate their needs and provide reassurance, the more quickly they will move on.

Understanding your child's unique qualities will help you to interact with them properly. For example, a child who is known for being quiet and shy might be pleased if you only talk to him or her after school. A bright light bulb over the head when he or she is bored can be a great icebreaker. On the other hand, an eccentric sibling with autism might not enjoy having a set time for reading every day. In fact, he or she may feel overwhelmed by activities that are go-go-go all the time (like doing homework).

Sensitive kids are adept at reading others' emotions, making them adept at interpreting those around them. If you want to reassure your child, don't just say it. Express your concern in terms that he or she can understand—say, "I know you are thinking…" If this is done right, the child will feel understood and feel safe enough to continue sharing what is on his or her mind.

Remember that highly sensitive children have a perfectly normal range of emotions and feelings. They cry when they need to and are happy when things go right for them. Emotional sensitivity is not a problem. To help your child develop emotional strength, it is necessary to let him or her know that you understand and accept these emotions.

Get your kids to understand the difference between their emotions and what other people may call "problems" or "anxiety." For example, if your child has been waiting for a few hours before he or she can go outside to play, don't ask "Are you anxious?" Instead, ask "Why do you want to go outside now?"

Just as it is important to understand the positives, some negatives must be addressed to ensure your child's well-being.

As you start to understand the qualities that make highly sensitive kids unique, you will see that they are often misunderstood. When they cry in class or are overly concerned about what other kids think, their behavior is seen by others as aloof or arrogant. This causes other children to bully and ostracize them and can lead to behavioral problems down the line. Parents should address this sensitive nature without giving up on the possibility of positive social interactions for their kids.

Parents of highly sensitive kids should realize that things will be different than what they had planned, but this is not a problem to be avoided. Instead of trying to avoid a situation that you know will make your child uncomfortable, look at it as an opportunity to learn something new. If you do this often enough over some time, your child will begin to gain confidence.

CHAPTER 1:

What Is High Sensitivity

Have you always been told that you are too sensitive for your own good, that you need to "toughen up," or that you cry too easily?

If you're a deep thinker who often feels as though you don't quite fit in, there's a good chance you might be an HSC.

This kind of sensitivity is more common than you might think. Dr. Elaine Aron, famous for her research with HSCs, states that approximately 20% of the population is highly sensitive.

Signs of the Highly Sensitive Person—A Helpful List

How many of the following describe you?

1. A tendency to feel particularly overwhelmed in noisy environments
2. A preference for smaller gatherings of people rather than large crowds
3. A good track record of picking up on other people's moods and motives
4. An ability to notice little changes in the environment
5. A tendency to be easily moved by music, books, films, and other media
6. Heightened sensitivity to hunger, pain, medication, and caffeine
7. A need to recharge and relax alone on a regular basis
8. An appreciation of good manners and politeness
9. Difficulty in refusing others' requests for fear of hurting their feelings
10. Difficulty in forgiving yourself for even the smallest mistakes
11. Perfectionism and imposter syndrome
12. Trouble handling conflict and criticism

You don't have to answer "Yes!" to every item on this list to qualify as an HSC. Trust your intuition. If this list resonates with you, there's a good chance that you have a highly sensitive personality.

D.O.E.S.—A Useful Way to Think about High Sensitivity

The D.O.E.S. model is a helpful acronym that explains the HSC profile.

- **Depth of processing:** HSCs have brains that work a little differently from the norm. They process incoming information—sights, sounds, smells, and so on—in a more thorough way. An HSC's mirror neurons—the cells in the brain that help us empathize with others—are more active than average. This explains why HSCs are especially sensitive to other people's moods and feelings and why they are readily overwhelmed in noisy places.

- **Overstimulation:** Overstimulation is inevitable when you have a particularly sensitive brain! An HSC takes longer than the average person to process stimuli, so they soon become overwhelmed and drained in busy or crowded environments. This also accounts for their heightened sensitivity to pain and hunger.
- **Emotional reactivity:** Emotional reactivity is probably what gets HSCs into trouble most often. They are always "tuned in" to their environment, so they cannot help but react strongly to both positive and negative situations. Unfortunately, their negative emotions can become all-consuming if not properly managed. Being so empathetic, they are also prone to picking up on other people's bad moods.
- **Sensing the subtle:** HSCs do not have superhuman powers—they see and hear just about as well as anyone else. However, they do have a special ability to pick up on tiny details in the environment that other people usually miss. For example, if you are an HSC, you may find that you are the first to notice when a vase of flowers has been moved to a different place in a room. This attention to detail also applies in social settings. An HSC can easily identify deception and ulterior motives in a friend or partner. Even when someone tries to conceal their true nature, an HSC will usually be able to see through the act!

High sensitivity isn't a disorder or an illness, it's just a natural variation that occurs in a minority of the human population. Men are just as likely to be highly sensitive as women, so don't assume that you can't be an HSC if you are a man.

HSC Myths

High sensitivity isn't well understood. Here are just a few of the most common myths… debunked:

- HSCs are empaths. All empaths are HSCs, but not all HSCs are empaths. You can think of an empath as an individual who meets all the criteria for high sensitivity yet has an additional set of abilities. An empath literally feels other people's emotions, whereas HSCs merely sense them. Empaths are also more vulnerable to negative energy and are more likely to report meaningful spiritual and intuitive experiences.
- HSCs are all introverts. While the majority of HSCs are introverts, almost one-third are actually extroverts! Don't dismiss the possibility that you are an HSC just because spending time with other people leaves you feeling energized rather than drained. In fact, HSCs can develop a wide circle of friends because they are so empathetic and intellectually stimulating.
- HSCs are just shy. HSCs often like to take their time when processing social situations, especially if they are in a noisy environment. To an outsider, their measured approach might suggest that they are shy. This isn't the case. It's more likely that a quiet HSC is just taking a moment or two to reflect on what is happening around them. They might appear slower to speak than others, but this is because they believe in the power of words and, therefore, prefer to think about what they want to say before opening their mouths.
- All HSCs have anxiety disorders and/or depression. This simply isn't true. High sensitivity describes a way of thinking and relating to the world, whereas anxiety disorders and depression are mental illnesses. However, HSCs can indeed become anxious and depressed if they don't understand their own needs. They also can experience great suffering if those

around them cannot, or will not, understand them. Later in this book, you'll learn how to keep yourself healthy and happy.
- All HSCs have Autism Spectrum Disorders (ASD). People with ASD sometimes have problems processing sensory information, and they can become overloaded as a result. In some cases, those with ASD can experience "meltdowns" triggered by excessive sensory input, so it's easy to see why people conflate "highly sensitive" and "autistic." However, there is a fundamental difference between being an HSC and having an ASD. An ASD is a developmental disorder, not a trait or personality type. To be diagnosed with ASD, an individual must show "persistent deficits in social communication and social interaction across multiple contexts." HSCs do not have problems communicating with other people, and the majority are skilled at social interaction.
- HSCs have Attention Deficit Hyperactivity Disorder (ADHD) or Attention Deficit Disorder (ADD), which is why they are so reactive to stimuli. This is simply untrue. ADHD and ADD are psychiatric disorders that usually require treatment, whereas high sensitivity is a natural variation that occurs in one-fifth of the population. This confusion arises because there are some points of similarity between HSCs and those with ADHD/ADD. Both groups tend to be perfectionists, they both have a well-developed sense of intuition, they both enjoy daydreaming, and they both like to help other people. They also share an appreciation for the arts, frequently feel the need to express themselves creatively, and believe in standing up for the oppressed. As an HSC, you may find that you naturally gravitate toward people with ADD or ADHD. However, there are a few signs that separate an HSC from someone with ADHD. For the most part, HSCs can concentrate for prolonged periods, which is usually a difficult task for those with ADHD. HSCs are usually better at following the thread of a conversation. However, an overstimulated HSC soon feels

overwhelmed, and they might find it hard to complete a task. To complicate matters further, it's possible to be highly sensitive and be diagnosed with ADHD or ADD at the same time! However, as a general rule, you are likely to be one or the other. Reading this book will help you gain clarity on this point. If you are still unsure, consider consulting a medical professional to obtain a definitive diagnosis.

- HSCs are rare. Twenty percent of the population are HSCs. You could argue that this makes them relatively unusual, but it's hardly a "rare" trait. To put it into perspective, at least one child in every classroom is an HSC, and there might be a few dozen working in a large company! Assuming you know at least five people besides yourself, there's a good chance you know another HSC.

- HSCs are more gifted, intelligent, or creative than the average person. This may or may not be true—we don't have enough information yet to know either way! Dr. Elaine Aron, a highly-regarded sensitivity expert, takes the view that HSCs and non-HSCs are probably equally as intelligent and creative.

- It's obvious when someone is highly sensitive. If you are an HSC, you probably have chosen to hide this trait from time to time. Most highly sensitive people have taught themselves to conceal their true nature for fear of being judged. For example, if your parents made you feel bad just because you happened to have a sensitive nature, it's almost inevitable that you would get into the habit of pretending to be "normal." As an HSC, you have been blessed with a strong sense of intuition, but don't beat yourself up if another HSC slips past you—over time, sensitive people can become highly accomplished at putting up a façade.

- HSCs can be "normal" if they want to change. An HSC can indeed act "normal," but this doesn't mean that they can turn their sensitivity on and off at will. They certainly don't choose to be more sensitive than the rest of the world.

- All HSCs prefer a quiet, boring life with little stimulation. Most HSCs value the opportunity to retreat from the hustle and bustle of the world to relax and recharge, particularly if they've had to spend a lot of time in a busy environment. However, this definitely does not mean that they want to stay at home all the time! HSCs tend to be curious about the world around them, so they will go out happily and explore it. Not only that, but extroverted HSCs can thrive in social situations that entail talking to lots of people.
- HSCs are weak. Sensitive doesn't mean "weak" or "frail." To survive as an HSC in a world that doesn't understand sensitivity requires strength and determination—in fact, you can't afford to be weak if you're an HSC!
- HSCs don't have successful careers. HSCs do have different requirements when it comes to the workplace. For example, as an HSC, you probably dislike jobs that require you to work in chaotic environments for hours at a time. However, as long as you understand and accommodate your needs, there is no reason you can't enjoy a great career. The key to having a successful career is identifying your strengths and making the most of them. For instance, as a diplomatic person who is reluctant to hurt anyone's feelings, you are in a great position to put forward constructive criticism and potentially controversial new ideas without causing undue offense. This will gain you respect at work. Later in this book, we'll look at how you can pick the perfect career for you.

There's a lot of information to take in when learning about high sensitivity. Fortunately, you don't have to remember all the finer details. Just bear in mind that, as an HSC, you can't help but process the world in a deeper, arguably more meaningful way than the majority of the population. Unfortunately, it's hard to manage your feelings if you don't have the tools to do so! Just because you feel emotions intensely doesn't mean you know how to deal with them.

CHAPTER 2:

How to Recognize a Highly Sensitive Child and Care for Him or Her

I Might Want to See Whether My Kid Is Highly Sensitive. Around What Percent of Children Are Highly Sensitive?

I don't have a clue the number of children, however, when I converse with different parents and ask the number of them who have a highly sensitive kid, they say generally a half. I've seen my kid doesn't care for schoolwork, likes to play without help from anyone else, and doesn't care for uproarious commotions, for example, vacuum cleaners, hairdryers, and so forth what would I be able to do about these things?

Parents ought not to feel remorseful that their children are brought into the world with an alternate disposition. This is because parents can't change their children's disposition and the personality of their children is frequently set by age three.

All in All, How Could Parents Adapt to Having a Sensitive Youngster?

Parents of Highly Sensitive Children will in general be more associated with their children's lives and regularly invest additional energy with their children on various exercises. This helps the kid with creating stronger methods for dealing with stress and builds up a nearer connection between the parent and youngster. It is significant that if you are highly sensitive, you figure out how to best adapt to your own affectability so you can help your children better as they become more established.

As I'm certain most parents would agree, how a parent reacts to a kid decides the personal satisfaction for their children. Significantly, parents of these children comprehend their kid's requirement for incessant sustaining and control. Make certain to request help if you need it.

You Would Say Highly Sensitive Children Are More Common in Young Men or Young Ladies?

It appears like young ladies are likelier to be highly sensitive than young men, presumably because they will in general be more sincerely insightful than young men who are frequently viewed as less genuinely astute than young ladies.

I Realize That a Few People Accept That Rising Has Almost No Impact on a Kid's Personality, Yet I Do Accept That Raising Affects a Kid's Personality. What Is Your Assessment on This?

I accept that rising hugely affects a youngster's personality. This is because children are given criticism and fortification of various practices by their parents. On the off chance that a parent is continually giving negative criticism, the kid will be bound to act as such.

My Highly Sensitive Kid Has Revealed to Me That He/She Doesn't Care for School. What Should Be Done About This?

If your kid discloses this to you, it could be a direct result of an additional heap of exercises planned at school during lunch or after school exercises. It will likewise rely on the personality of the instructor just as the climate of the classroom if it is excessively boisterous or having such a large number of people in there talking, and so forth.

What Is the Normal Time of Children Who Are Distinguished as Highly Sensitive?

Numerous parents don't understand that their youngster is highly sensitive until after their kid turns into an adult. Normally when a youngster hits adolescence parents start to see that their kid will withdraw from social exercises and become less and less associated with different children.

Numerous children start to encounter tactile over-burden right now. It isn't remarkable for SEN children (SEN represents Sensory Processing Disorder) to feel so overpowered by sounds, lights, contact, and so forth… that they may even start to hurt themselves or others out of sheer dissatisfaction.

Some might be ascribed to changes in the kid's chemicals, which have now enacted the fight-or-run reaction making them need to run or battle whatever is causing them uneasiness. Sounds familiar?

This is the reason it is so critical to instruct parents of Highly Sensitive Children at an early age so a solid and gainful relationship can be set up with parents, educators, partners, and others. It is safe to say that you are mindful of any assets accessible for SEN children?

Numerous schools have language instructors accessible who can perform screenings on SEN children. They would then be able to suggest the best treatment if fundamental. There are numerous books composed on Sensory Processing Disorder by Elaine N. Aron Ph.D., M.S.

CHAPTER 3:

Tips if Your Newborn Cries Too Much

You've just given birth to a beautiful, new baby and you're enjoying every last moment with them. But there comes a time when your newborn can't seem to stop crying and the constant noise is driving you mad.

If you're stuck in this predicament, we've put together this chapter all about tips for if your newborn cries too much! We break down what could be causing the incessant wailing, as well as what you can do about it. You'll find that most of these solutions are easy fixes that require minimal effort on your part (and will probably do wonders for your sanity too).

When it comes to newborns, there are a plethora of reasons why they could be crying so much. The good thing is that most of the time the solution is pretty simple. Before we go into the solutions for your crying baby, let's take a look at some of the common reasons for your constantly wailing newborns.

Common Reasons for Crying

Here are some common reasons why you might have a wailing baby on your hands:

1. Hungry: If your baby has been fed recently and they're still bawling, then chances are that they're just hungry again! Just like adults, when babies get hungry they'll start to grumble and complain until the food arrives. One thing to remember is that they're not going to be able to express their needs verbally, so you'll need to use other methods to find out what they want.

2. Colds: The common cold in babies is completely natural and absolutely nothing to worry about (you can read more about common colds in babies here). If your baby has a mild sniffle or seems congested, take them into the bathroom and bath them with warm water mixed with coconut oil (as opposed to tap water). Afterward, gently pat their chest until their congestion starts clearing up.
3. Colics: Newborns with colic will cry for extended periods (yes, it's a bummer). The good news is that colic only tends to last for the first 3-4 months after birth. During this time, you can help reduce the amount of crying by swaddling your baby in a soft blanket and putting them in a dark, quiet room with no lights or bright colors.
4. Transitioning: Babies who are just used to the comfort of their mother's womb will tend to get very cranky when they're forced to transition into life outside of mommy's tummy. As soon as their new surroundings start to become more comfortable, they'll start to settle in and your screaming baby should stop. If you're worried that your newborn is having trouble with this, try giving them a pacifier or nursing them on your chest at night. This will help give them a sense of comfort in the transition period.

What to Do

1. Swaddle: The first thing you can do is try swaddling your child to calm down their wailing. By putting them in a soft sleeping bag, bib, or piece of cloth they'll feel more secure and will be less likely to cry so much anyway.
2. Find out what they want: The most important thing is to find out what they want. If your child hasn't been fed recently, they'll keep crying until you give them some food (remember, no verbal skills yet). If your child isn't hungry, try giving them a bottle with warm water or even a pacifier. Pacifiers tend to be the best choice if you're looking for something to calm the baby and put him to sleep because it will help them associate

sucking with comfort which will encourage them to fall asleep and stay asleep longer.
3. Get moving: Babies tend to like movement and if yours doesn't, then you can rock or sway them until they stop crying. If you have an exercise ball, you can also bounce them on it gently, or even set up a baby swing so they can swing back and forth to calm them down.
4. Lighten the mood: If your baby's crying because of something that isn't urgent (such as transition), try to lighten the mood with books, music, or even bath time. Some babies will have a sense of security with being read to or played music and singing will cause their brain waves to calm down.

Other Tips

1. Cell phone: It's a shame that we do it to ourselves but we all get attached to our cell phones in ways that we don't realize until someone else takes them away from us. If they're less than a week old, you'll find that your baby will be just as attached to their cell phone (it's normal). If you're worried that this attachment is becoming unhealthy then consider installing a baby monitor on the wall so your child can hear you (and vice versa) while you take care of other things around the house.
2. Take 10: The hardest thing for any parent is to put their child down and walk away because it's impossible to do so without a good reason. There are times when you might need to do this though and one of those times is if they're constantly screaming at night. If your baby is less than a month old, try turning on some music (or even vacuum) so they don't get used to hearing the same sounds. If you can't do this, tummy time is also very important for your child's development (for example). While it may be hard to do so, be sure to take 10 away from your child because you should have other things going on in your life that will help you become a better person.

3. Baby playdates: If you're having trouble with any of these tips and you simply want someone else to babysit your child then consider the idea of baby playdates as well. If you're an adult that is learning how to better watch your child, then consider hiring an older babysitter that can help you with any of these tips.

CHAPTER 4:

2 to 6 Months

Tips on How to Manage Overstimulation

Many parents find themselves in the most difficult situation when their HSCs are between the ages of 2 and 6 months. This is because babies have so much to explore and they always want to touch everything. They start doing things like grabbing for objects or crawling on the floor, which often leads to overstimulation when it comes time to put them down for a nap.

Sometimes parents report that babies around this age are fussy and irritable during the day. It is also a time when the baby's brain is rapidly developing, which means that they are constantly taking in new sights, sounds, and smells. This can be very stimulating for them, which may result in an overstimulated baby. However, there are some tricks you can use to help reduce overstimulation.

- The first step is to understand what exactly is being overstimulated. It is well known that overstimulation can include low-level lights, high-frequency sounds, and even the feel of specific materials. Some babies are more sensitive than others, so it is best to take note of specific things that upset your baby.
- To help reduce overstimulation, try to limit the number of senses being stimulated at any one time. For example, if your baby is fussy in a store when you are trying to shop, you can take him or her outside since they won't be exposed to as many sounds as they would be in a store. You can also control their exposure to lights and other visual stimuli by keeping

them in a shaded area like under an umbrella or by covering their eyes with a cloth.
- Similarly, you can control how much your HSC can touch things. For example, if your HSC is crawling on the floor, try to limit which objects he or she is touching. You could also move a specific toy out of his or her reach if it is a favorite, then put it back later. Another trick is to purchase toys that are made of soft fabric instead of hard metals like spoons and plasters. This will decrease the chances that they will chew on them.
- If you find that your baby always seems overstimulated, then it might be a good idea to keep some activities on hand that will help him or her focus on something else and calm down. For example, you can play music near the crib while your baby is napping so he or she can listen to it while they drift off to sleep. You can also have a toy nearby for them to play with when they are awake too. Try purchasing some new toys that are soft and made of materials like cloth so they won't hurt themselves by chewing on them.
- When it comes to feeding time, try only offering one type of food at a time. Some babies develop a preference for certain foods or textures, so giving them too many different things at once can cause them to be overstimulated. That is why you want to make sure that they are getting enough protein and calcium from their formula. If your baby is not eating well, then it may be worth taking him or her to the doctor since he or she may have reflux or other health-related problems.
- If your baby suffers from overstimulation for longer than two months, then you might want to consider sleeping your baby in a different room from the rest of the family. This is especially true for families who have a new baby and don't want to overstimulate them. You can also try placing your baby in a bassinet. This way you will still be nearby, but your baby can feel more secure since they won't be alone.

- You might also try using a noise machine or some other type of appliance that emits a steady sound that will help put your HSC's mind at ease when he or she wakes up at night. These devices can block out distracting noises from outside and help the baby fall back asleep faster. Plus, you won't have to worry about waking up when the baby cries since you'll hear the noise machine as well.
- You may also want to consider swaddling your baby when he or she is napping or sleeping at night. This will help them feel more secure and develop better sleep habits. You can find instructions online for how to do this properly and safely so you don't accidentally cause harm to your baby.

If you are thinking about having more children, then it might be a good idea to postpone that until your HSC is older. It often takes babies a few months to recover from the effects of overstimulation, so it's best if you wait until they are doing better before trying again. You can even wait until your HSC is at least 3 years old since that is when most HSCs can tolerate more stimuli.

Now that you know what to look for when your baby has been overstimulated, you will be able to spot the signs that something's wrong and get him or her help sooner rather than later. Remember, though, that sometimes babies will grow out of it on their own so if your baby's symptoms persist then speak with a doctor to see if they can help.

Tips on How to Manage Sleep Problems

As babies grow, their sleep needs change. But the way we've been parenting for those first six months just doesn't work anymore. We're not sure what to do!

You're not alone in this struggle: It turns out that most parents have a hard time figuring out how much sleep their baby needs at this age.

But it's a very important time: Your baby needs lots of sleep during this phase to develop.

First off—remember that no matter how deeply your HSC sleeps, she needs at least 10 hours of sleep in 24 hours.

What Kind of Sleep Does a Baby Need?

The first three months of life are the time for getting your baby used to sleep on a regular schedule. She'll sleep in short bursts, and you have to respect this to help her develop healthy sleep patterns.

After that, she'll begin sleeping longer stretches at night and take naps during the day. You'll notice your baby gradually spending more time in each phase of sleep—starting out with rapid-eye-movement (REM) periods lasting only seconds, as compared to longer periods of non-REM sleep. By six months old, REM periods last 15–20 minutes.

Whether your baby's sleep is deep or light, she continues to need the same amount of sleep. She'll also need to be on the same schedule every night.

When Should My Baby Start Sleeping Through the Night?

A baby's brain isn't fully developed until he's about 2 years old, so for most babies, daytime naps play a big part in helping him get much-needed daytime rest. But when he does take a nap, he needs at least one full sleep cycle so that his brain will know it's time to go back to sleep and not wake up again.

Here's what this looks like

Babies sleep through the night for every nap in a regular cycle, and then they'll wake up between 3 p.m. and 6 p.m., depending on their age and how much sleep they got the night before. Then they'll put themselves back to bed, get about 2–3 hours of sleep, wake up several hours later around 8–9 p.m., and go back to sleep until it's time for their next nap (about 4 a.m.). They probably won't take another full night-time nap until after their first birthday—when they're ready for longer naps—unless there are developmental issues that prevent them from going back to sleep.

If your baby isn't napping well, or not napping at all, he must get a good night's sleep so he'll be rested and ready to play in the morning.

What Doesn't Work When It Comes to Your Baby's Sleep?

- Crying it out: If you want to let your HSC cry himself to sleep, now is the time to choose another method. Crying yourself out as a baby can make you anxious and fearful as an adult; it can also make you tired.
- Sleep associations: To get your baby used to falling asleep on her own, give her lots of time in active awake play. Make sure you put her in bed awake and then respect her sleep. Remember, she needs at least 10 hours of sleep in 24 hours.
- "Sleep crutches": When you're putting your baby to bed, don't use things like rocking, car rides, patting, or smelling a certain scent to help him fall asleep. If he's crying a lot when you try to put him down awake, check in with your pediatrician; his cries might mean that he's hungry, has gas or reflux (which is common at this age), or is uncomfortable for another reason.

What Works When It Comes to Your Infant's Sleep?

- Deep sleep: S-shaped patterns of deep sleep are the best for this age, which means starting your baby's nighttime sleep with at least four hours of deep sleep. This is what she needs to get ready for a solid night's rest.
- Baby sleeping in his own crib: Nothing disrupts your baby's deep sleep more than being woken up by a soft thud from someone touching or jiggling his crib.
- Sleep positioners: They're great for cradling your baby close during the night, and they're also good at keeping her from rolling over too much while she sleeps. This is because sleep

positioners restrict your baby's movement. Keep in mind that your baby needs to be able to roll over from her stomach to her back. Don't use a sleep positioner when she's awake, so she can get used to moving around while in bed.

- Sleep training: If you want your baby's sleep patterns to stick, try a structured routine of nighttime sleep. You can work with a trained professional or on your own with the book The Happiest Baby on the Block. Pay attention to your baby's behavior and limit his "awake" time in bed, so that he'll be more likely to go back to sleep on his own.

CHAPTER 5:

1 to 5 Years. Pre-School age. At Home

Managing HSC at Home

All parents worry about their kids, but they can be more anxious, tender-hearted, and sensitive than most. A high-sensitive child is naturally more emotional and sensitive to sensory input, which can make them look fussy or whiny in public places. Here are some tips for managing a high-sensitive child at home:

- Clothes: Choose clothes that are lightweight and soft to the touch (consider natural fibers). Swaddling may help babies with rapid eye movement sleep better.
- Food: Serve a wide variety of fresh foods, especially raw vegetables. Avoid processed and restaurant foods. Some high-sensitive children may react to smells, flavors, textures, and colors in their food. Consider holding off on meat until one year of age or later for kids who can't handle the taste or texture.
- Toilet training: Toilet training can be a big challenge for sensitive kids, who can have anxiety about losing control in public restrooms. They're also extra sensitive to odors in these places and might not like wiping themselves with wet wipes among other toiletry items that smell strongly and be avoided at home if possible. Help your child to understand when it is time to go potty. Get him or her to point to the toilet. Praise your child when he or she goes. (e.g., "Wow, you are so good at telling the time.") Talk about body parts and good bathroom habits.

- Touching genitals: Many high-sensitive children have difficulty with genital touching, which can negatively affect their enjoyment of bathing, using the toilet, and changing their clothes. Consider a "clean up" routine that doesn't require touching private parts.
- Nightmares: About half of all kids have nightmares, but high sensitivity is one reason why some kids can have more than one night per week with frequent night terrors or nightmares. Some parents can comfort kids back to sleep while others might need to wake up their kids several times a week for months to help them learn how to fall back asleep without parental assistance.
- Eating out: Kids with high sensitivity can sometimes have intense reactions to odors, tastes, and textures in restaurant settings. Try not to eat at restaurants that are known for being too noisy or smelly. More...
- Bedroom: A child's bedroom can create sensory overload and lead to fear, anxiety, and nightmares. Look for quiet colors and soft textures for bedding, fabrics, and decoration. Consider having a calming bath ritual before bedtime to help children relax.
- Traveling: If your child has a hard time sleeping on car trips, look for travel pillows or consider a more sound-proofed vehicle as to the best option. While you're driving, talk to kids about where you are going, why you're going there, and what you'll be doing when you arrive.

In many ways, a high-sensitive child is like a high-performance athlete or a musician who has to practice their craft for hours every day to get better. Kids need lots of sleep and downtime (in their own rooms) to recover from the day and improve their abilities at school.

Encourage the Reflective Nature of the HSC

Highly sensitive children are more perceptive of their surroundings and show greater awareness in reaction to sensory stimuli. This trait is linked to a higher capacity for empathy and compassion, which makes them ideal leaders in the future. Encourage the reflective nature of these children by:

- Offering routines that allow them time to reflect on their day.
- Creating an atmosphere where one can escape from excessive noise or activity.
- Permitting them to take care of themselves when they need it most.
- Instilling self-reliance at an early age so they are not dependent on supervision all the time.

As a parent, it can be easy to give in and let your child discover these things on their own. Social engineering is the term coined by social engineers for changing behaviors through coercion, manipulation, illusion, or deceit. The first step to self-discovery is realizing that it cannot be forced and that the path will find itself naturally.

It can be easy to give in and let your child discover these things on their own as they are naturally curious about the world around them. While this might seem like a negative trait for certain industries (such as advertising) this could actually create a skill for them to use later in life.

Encouraging the reflective nature of the highly sensitive child will provide them with a trait that can aid in their social interaction and help them in their relationships. This is beneficial for an engineering career because these are people who take in and assimilate information easily. This can also be beneficial to their personal success as they are more likely to consider the needs of others and realize that everyone needs help from time to time.

Parents may find it very difficult to understand why their children are so sensitive or why they feel so overwhelmed by minor things, but this is just part of what makes them special. These children will be able to notice and absorb information easily as they are more perceptive and observant. This allows them to see the world in a whole new way and realize the importance of life and relationships.

It can be easy for parents to tell their children what is right or wrong, but this does not always work overtime since these children often become accustomed to being told what to do.

Children's reactions can also be more dramatic as it takes a lot more for them to feel aggravated or angry. For example, if their child gets upset because their favorite toy has been broken they might scream very loudly to get their attention back when you would normally react by scolding them quietly.

Parents can help their children to learn by exercising patience, understanding, and listening to them.

Children's moods may be very extreme and this can often place a lot of stress on their parents as well as the whole family. If this becomes a problem the parent must become more aware of their child's temperament traits to try and understand why they act the way they do. An easy way to ensure you are not overreacting is by giving yourself a warning period before getting upset or angry at them.

Being "extremely" sensitive can also make it difficult for children to express themselves in certain situations because of how easily they get overwhelmed or upset. The parents can help the child to express their feelings healthily and positively by similarly expressing themselves.

Being good at drawing or painting can be beneficial for these more sensitive children, as it allows them to observe and visualize the world around them. In this way, they will become more aware of their surroundings and able to learn. This is also useful because it teaches them how to be creative which is a very important skill for everyone.

The parents should also encourage their child's creativity by providing them with a space where they can make art whenever they wish. This should also include helping the child to learn how to draw properly and in a way that looks good.

It is also a good idea to allow the child their own special space where they can be alone when they want. This will allow them to discover for themselves what it is like to be in a place without people around and understand what this feels like. Every sensitive person needs to have their own space at home where they know no one will bother them, such as a room of their own.

High sensitivity is linked with mental problems such as anxiety and depression, but this does not mean that each sensitive child experiences these things or that they are going through the same problem at the same time. These children may also be more likely to be bullied or teased by others because of their sensitivity, so the parents must talk to them about what they can do in these situations.

If their child is extremely sensitive then they might experience a lot of stress when it comes to social situations. For example, they may feel pressure from peers who want them to fit into a certain kind of group or act in a certain way that is different from how they feel comfortable acting. Guidance and reassurance as well as being involved in their child's life on a day-to-day basis can help with this issue.

High sensitivity is not a problem, but it does mean that the child will experience a lot of emotional changes throughout their life. They may struggle with a difficult home life or problems at school, and they might have difficulty making friends due to their shyness and over-sensitivity to others' emotions. The parents should be understanding of these situations and be supportive in any way they can.

CHAPTER 6:

1 to 5 years. Pre-school. Outside the Home

How to Support the HSC When Entering the World

If you're a sensitive person, chances are your children are more sensitive too. Sensitive people often react more strongly to external stimuli, and as a result, may require more support. It can be difficult to know how best to provide this support when the sensitivities of the sensitive child are misunderstood in our society. The following is some advice on supporting high-sensitivity children from educators who work with them every day:

1. Fostering their strengths and interests: Sensitive children tend to gravitate towards activities that meet their needs, rather than those that provide them with the most "bang for their buck. They may be drawn to music, art, or writing. They may also enjoy nature and spending time in solitude. Encourage these interests as a way of supporting your child's sensitive temperament.
2. Finding balance: Sensitive children need to find a balance between their own unique needs and the expectations of others. They need encouragement to express themselves, but might also benefit from limits and discipline to help them feel secure. Maintain a balance between creative expression and direct instruction through healthy limits, consistent rules and practical expectations.
3. Encouraging their strengths in school: Sensitive children tend not to be "cool" kids, which can make them vulnerable targets for teasing and bullying at school. It can be easy to respond to this by withdrawing the child from school altogether. Instead,

encourage school-based activities that support the child's unique strengths and interests.
4. Encouraging their uniqueness in other areas of their life: Sensitive children are often very private people who struggle to explain themselves and find it hard to relate with others. They tend not to have close friends and can become isolated in a world that doesn't understand them. Encourage your child to spend time alone, but also offer opportunities for friendships and playmates outside of school.
5. Re-establishing connections with their family and others: Sensitive children often have a hard time "letting themselves go" in social situations. Instead, they tend to withdraw into an inner world of their own making. This can make it hard for them to build and keep relationships, especially with their families. Encourage them to spend time alone or with others in the privacy of their home and bedrooms.
6. Creating a safe haven: Sensitive children may have an almost perpetually anxious temperament that makes them more prone to being overwhelmed by emotional stimuli such as noise, crowds, or conflict. These children need lots of encouragement and support to develop a safety zone in their life that allows them to escape their innate sensitivity. They often need a haven where they can be alone, such as their bedroom, or a place outside of the house to retreat to. They may also benefit from calming techniques like deep breathing exercises, or other coping mechanisms that help them to de-stress in other situations.
7. Providing a healthy diet and lifestyle: Sensitive children tend not to respond well when they become overly stressed and tend to "blow" easily. They need the stimulation that is more predictable than that offered by video games and television but may also have trouble handling the sugar rush provided by sugary treats and candy. Provide your child with a balanced diet that includes enough protein, complex carbohydrates, and

fiber. While sweets can be a temptation, try to limit the amount you'll give them.
8. Re-establishing boundaries: Sensitive children are often very sensitive to "too much," both in new situations and in their everyday lives. They need to learn how to set limits and feel safe doing so without fear of punishment, blame, or judgment. Encourage them to pace themselves, and build up expectations before they get overwhelmed.
9. Giving the child space: Sensitive children often need a lot of their own space depending on the situation. This can be helpful if they are doing things that are stimulating or overwhelming for them such as dealing with a new environment. However, it is also a way for the child to cope with overstimulation. Give them space to be alone and retreat to their safe place when they need it.
10. Encouraging a strong sense of self: Sensitive children tend not to do well in tasks that require them to be confrontational or rely on aggressive behavior. While this may make them seem "passive" at times, they are expressing themselves in a different way than other children are. Encourage your child to stand up for him or herself whenever possible, but don't expect them to do so through aggression or defiance. Instead, help them find their own unique voice.
11. Exploring their sensitivities: Highly sensitive Children often benefit from learning how to describe their responses and help themselves to manage them. This can be done through some form of visualization, dance, or yoga. While this method is not scientifically proven, it does help teach the child how to calm themselves and manage their own reactions.
12. Helping them be present: Highly sensitive children may find it hard to focus on tasks that require intense concentration or full attention. Encourage them to give attention to more subtle experiences like sounds and images rather than allowing

themselves to become overwhelmed by too much information at once.
13. Encouraging them to connect with others: Sensitive children usually have a hard time making social connections and may lack the self-confidence to try and make friends. Help your child find things they enjoy doing, both in the real world and through media such as books, games, or movies that allow them to relate with other characters in a safe way.
14. Supporting their creative side: Sensitive children often show a tremendous capacity for creativity but may struggle to express themselves in creative ways. Help them figure out ways to express themselves through art or other forms of self-expression like music or dance.
15. Finding their role in the family: Sensitive children may struggle to find their place in the family and feel overshadowed by more dominant personalities. Try to give them tasks that don't involve conflict, but allow them to be helpful and use their talents.

Social Shyness, Trying New Things, Kindergarten

There's no denying that socializing can be hard and awkward. But for too many children, social shyness is actually the norm and they don't learn the skills to help them navigate difficult social interactions. Yet, even if your child is not one of these children, it doesn't mean they shouldn't be allowed to try new things and have fun!

Here are some tips that can help prevent social shyness and foster the healthy development of social skills:

- Make sure they are getting plenty of sleep. If they start the day with a nap, they'll be less tired, which will make it easier for them to go out and try new things. They'll also be more focused in class and better able to make friends. Here's the real clincher... allow naps until around 5 years old, which is when kids become too active to micro-sleep well.

- Don't put limits on what they wear or say. Dress them in whatever is comfortable and keep communications clear.
- Pick them up and say "I love you!" when you see them. It might not seem like much, but if you can get them to recognize the simple words of love, they'll remember it when they feel more vulnerable.
- Have an open discussion with your child about what makes someone popular, including why people like or dislike someone. This will help your child understand that other people have different ideas about popularity than they do themselves.
- Start your own group of friends, where everyone can choose the best friend and peer pressure will not be a problem. You may choose to rotate this among friends or keep the same set of friends.
- Don't push your child to play with others, when they are uncomfortable. This can reinforce their anxiety and make them feel like they are doing something wrong. Let them know that they can take a break from socializing if they want to, but that you still love them.
- Be a role model for your child by showing them how you handle difficult people or social situations. Include yourself in your list of people your child can call when he/she needs support or advice about school or changing friends.
- Make sure your child understands that there's a difference between being shy and being introverted. Being shy usually means that your child wants to engage in social interactions but is having a hard time with it. Introversion tends not to be caused by shyness. It's an emotion that allows for quiet or introverted activities but does not involve being standoffish or uninterested.

So now that you know what causes social shyness, here are some things you can do to help your child overcome this:

- Make sure your child has an adult they can go to if the situation gets too overwhelming. Sometimes it's better to make a quick exit, rather than stay and feel more anxiety.
- Make sure your child has short, simple routines that they follow to help them feel set in a comfortable and safe world. Permit them to do something they enjoy when it's not time for school or play so that they know what to expect when the going gets tough.
- Give them time and space to have fun and be themselves. This will help them feel more secure being themselves around you or their other friends.
- If your child is getting teased, talk with your child about it later at home instead of trying to fix it immediately on the playground or in class. Explain that being teased is an uncomfortable feeling and doesn't mean you are a bad person at all. Sometimes kids say mean things to make themselves feel more important. Either way, it's not nice to be teased, but you can handle it.
- Give your child permission to say "no" if they want to, for any situation that they feel uncomfortable or unable to handle. This will help them deal with the anxiety associated with saying "no" and give them an alternative option if they're feeling pressured into doing something they don't want to do.
- Helping your child in social situations doesn't necessarily mean forcing him/her to do what the other kids are doing, but helping them adjust and find a way that works for them.
- If your child is reluctant to try new things (like riding a bicycle), then they might need some help transitioning from the things they like to the new activity. This will help them feel more comfortable in both situations and make it easier for them to engage with new activities. Offer your support and encouragement, but don't push too hard, as this can start to make your child feel overwhelmed or anxious.

When Should I Start My Child on These Skills?

Children usually learn social skills between two and four years of age. However, some children may not know how to respond when someone compliments them or wants to play with them at their age. You can start working on these skills as soon as you (or your child) can understand them.

When Should I Stop My Child from Working on These Skills?

Once a child has learned the social skills necessary for living in a safe and comfortable world, I would continue to work with that skill set until they are about seven years old, when they should be ready to move into a more independent social environment, without help from an adult.

Once your child understands social cues and can work independently with other children, it's time to introduce other areas of life such as school, friends, or play dates... again without your adult help.

Arrange with School

Make your youngster's school your partner. They are inclined to be harassed and you can't be there the entire chance to look after them or to avoid their domineering jerks. In such a manner, the school turns into another parent and has the obligation regarding your children while they are nearby. To help your kid, get input from your kid's educator. The educator is the best person who knows your youngster since the person sees your kid during the greater part of the day. They know class elements and how your kid adapts to the various burdens. They are then in the best situation to give target criticism on your kid. They will answer to you if your kid is being pained and how the individual in question is taking care of the circumstance. The objective here isn't to place a camera in the classroom, however, to search out a partner in framing children.

Instruct your educators about what a highly sensitive kid is. This isn't to request extraordinary treatment or even to make instructors feel sorry for your kid.

CHAPTER 7:

HSC ages 5 and 12. In School-Age. At home and Out of Home

Give HSC Social Skills to Live in the World

Highly sensitive children are intelligent and conscientious. They make wonderful friends and can be helpful and empathetic creatures. But children with this trait can have trouble living in the world. As adults, they like to live alone or at least away from noise and activity; as kids, they often find themselves socially isolated, disliked by their peers, bullied, or teased mercilessly for being different.

Include Them in Housework

Housework is particularly developmental for HSCs. Include them in family unit tasks that they are prepared to do. They may at first deny and go into fits of rage. Be that as it may, when they see your emphasis on the family errands, they will follow. From the accompanying, they can figure out how these little demonstrations can benefit them as they fill in autonomy from their parents. Allow them to work it out as they tidy up their room so they can value the estimation of difficult work.

Allow them to wash dishes so they can gain proficiency with the estimation of cleanliness. Allow them to get their toys and put them in the right place so they can be liable for dealing with their own things. At the point when you do these errands together, you are in any event, disclosing to them that they are important for the family. HSCs can act naturally retained and when they are drawn out by finishing errands, they can understand how similarly significant it is to get things done with others.

Set Up Rules

At the point when you set out the principles, you are showing your children the benefit of keeping limits. These limits are not intended to make your kids awkward or to subdue their opportunities. Or maybe, these limits are intended for them to have a good time in the best and most benefit able manner conceivable. Parents struggle with setting up and implementing rules since often they experienced childhood in families that either have no guidelines or are too exacting principles.

Our own insight of house rules will really decide the sort of rules we will implement in our home. Be that as it may, since a few of us have terrible encounters of training, it is ideal to comprehend what sort of rules will work best.

One nature of a standard is that it should be clear. At the point when parents tell their children any standard, the standard should be clear and depicted. On the off chance that you tell your children that they ought to be home around evening time, they will be exceptionally confounded. Does it imply that they must be in the house when it gets dim? Would they be able to extend it to 12 PM? Is 4 AM actually viewed as night? However, if you plan your standard as they ought to be home by 6 PM; at that point, the standard turns out to be clear. Obscure decisions will be liable to a lot of understandings and you will end up getting protective and dictator.

The second quality of a decent standard is that it ought to be sensible. Your standard should bode well, even to a youngster. The most exceedingly awful thing a parent can say to their children when inquired as to why the children ought to do an errand is that "since I say as much." This is said when parents are depleted to show their children the reason behind the assignment or the task they are being made to do. As parents, we ought to put forth a valiant effort to disclose to our children why we do the things we do to the limit that they can comprehend.

At the point when you advise them to make up their bed, you need to clarify the estimation of tidiness and having an arranged room and not simply dismiss the inquiry with "Get it done." When they ask you for what reason they need to quit sitting in front of the TV or play computer games following 60 minutes, give a valiant effort to disclose to them the estimation of time the executives and in any event, separating from gadgets to collaborate with genuine individuals. They won't comprehend everything at the same time.

However, when you are not protective and children see that they can ask you inquiries without being dismissed, the accompanying rules get simpler.

The last quality of a decent guideline is that it ought to be imparted unmistakably. You don't imagine administers on the spot when it is helpful for you. You don't force decisions that no one but you can comprehend.

These are as clear as day, yet you would be astounded at how helpless a few parents can be in disclosing rules to their children. In their brain, they definitely realize that they have advised their children not to contact or utilize their personal things. In any case, in truth, they have just murmured it off in passing or clarified it in dubious terms. At the point when their children alter their personal things, they fly into a fierceness and the children can get damaged. You need to ensure that you express your standards in a way that is reasonable to your children. Request that they repeat your standard after you said it. Test if they truly recall your guidelines. You can teach them when they have perceived your standard and still disregarded it. In any case, up to that point, you can't make them liable for defying guidelines you have not imparted appropriately.

The following part of setting up principles is authorizing. You don't simply cause rules and not follow them up with execution. Decisions are there so the children will keep them. At the point when you authorize rules, you must be firm.

They possibly become rules when children sense your clout in upholding them. If you say the time limitation is at 6 PM, it is 6 PM, not 6:30 PM, not 7 PM. If you emphatically feel that these are rules your children will require later on throughout everyday life, at that point, start them ahead of schedule with discipline.

They will require a decent arrangement of rules to carry on appropriately. Like some other kid, they will submit missteps and defy a few norms. Have a go at disclosing outcomes to them so they can take negative input appropriately. Try not to be delicate on them since they will be tough eventually. Simply ensure that your order is proportionate to the measure of taking in they can get from the discipline. Recall that the objective of control isn't to rebuff, but to show children how to act appropriately.

Energize Open Communication

At the point when children submit a blunder or defy a norm, there is a propensity to conceal it from parents since they will be rebuffed. They may have encounters where you burst out of resentment or you even genuinely hit them since they submitted an infraction. Try not to damage your children. There ought to be a solid way to deal with submitting botches so you actually will address the conduct however at the equivalent, empower open correspondence. Zero in on the demonstration that you need to right and not on the person who submitted it. Disclose to your youngster that you are pulling out advantages, not because an individual is an awful person, but since what he did was bad. By depersonalizing the conduct, you can in any case stretch out your affection to your kid and, simultaneously, discipline that person. Next time, children will feel that they can answer their mix-ups and own up to them. This as of now means that they are getting liable for their activities and are available to accept the outcomes. The remedial interaction at that point gets developmental for your children.

Have a Dialogue About Overstimulation

One of the most confusing and difficult parts of raising a highly sensitive child is their intense aversion to overstimulation. What do you do when your sensitive kid just can't get enough downtime in between all the other responsibilities for their day? This dialogue tackles that very issue and suggests some ways to give them the break they need without it impacting other aspects of their life too much.

Q. My son is 7, and quite sensitive to stimuli. He loves music but hates loud noises. He loves nature and animals but gets overloaded by certain types of smells. Hugs are fine, but standing too close makes him uncomfortable (he doesn't like to be touched). I don't know how to help him cope with this overstimulation—he gets depressed when he can't be around his friends or go to his favorite places (like the pet store or the art store), and he has trouble sitting still in school. The school will only accommodate him if I have a doctor's note. I'm reluctant to start the process of getting him an official diagnosis because it seems like that might just add to his problems. What can I do to help him manage overstimulation?

A. First, you are right to be reluctant about getting him officially diagnosed with HSC, as this is not required and could actually end up creating more problems for your son. He may already be sensitive, and you have found some ways to cope with it. So this might not be such a big deal in his life. You know he is sensitive, and that he needs time alone.

Let's take a look at your suggestions:

1. Music he doesn't like: Take him to the music store and let him try all sorts of instruments (drum set, guitar, piano, saxophone). Help him identify which instruments he likes (maybe a ukulele). It is helpful to have two instruments, one for at home and one for carrying around. Get a ukulele and a keyboard, so he can get used to them. He may also want headphones, helpful if some types of music are too loud.
2. Nature/animals: Take him to the library and have him read all sorts of books about nature, animals, and animals in the wild (his favorite). He should also learn more about animals: what they eat, how they survive in the wild. Make sure to talk with him about his feelings about different animals.
3. Smells: Find pens that you like the smell of and let him sniff them. Go to a pet store or an herb shop and talk about the smells. Play memory games where he has to remember smells. You can get t-shirts from the store with various smells.
4. Hugs: Give him lots of hugs, and be sure to touch him more often than before (hold hands, hug him when you say hello/goodbye, touch his back when you want to have a conversation).
5. Overstimulation in school: Talk with your son's teacher about what happens when he gets overstimulated in class (does he move around a lot? does he have problems focusing on the work?). Also, talk with his teacher about how to help him stay in the moment and focus on the work. Ask for a "time out" if he gets to the point where he is over-stimulated in class.

It will be more effective to get him some help with his overstimulation since it will help him to cope with this part of his life better. Be sure you have a family meeting about this, and see what the teachers think about it as well. Don't hesitate to cut back on some of his activities (music, art classes, animals), or schedule less time for them so they can fit into your life better.

Another problem with sensitivity is that it can create problems for your son, such as isolation. It is also common for sensitive kids to get teased. Be sure to talk to your child's teacher about this. You might also want to get an evaluation from a psychiatrist or psychologist who specializes in the HSC population if you are worried about other issues too. It will be more helpful than just understanding him better by getting him diagnosed at all.

What Is Going On? Why Do HSCs Seem So Different From Other People?

Some psychologists believe that HSCs are somehow predisposed to a neurobiological vulnerability that makes them more likely to experience strong and unpleasant affective states of mind. Others think that the difference is simply that HSC children are raised in homes and communities where they're not encouraged to develop relationships with others, and therefore learn to avoid being around other people. Either way, most agree that HSCs, with or without autism, have a difficult time managing what they're feeling.

In the last few years, a psychological model called the Emotion Regulation Index (EREI) has emerged as one approach for understanding this phenomenon. It has led to some effective interventions which are being used with increasing frequency in schools and homes in the US.

This approach provides us with an additional focus for understanding what's going on and for helping children learn to handle their own emotional experiences and to develop more successful social relationships.

The EREI model describes emotion regulation as a set of three skills:

1. The ability to identify, label and describe one's own feelings
2. The ability to modulate one's negative affect

3. The ability to initiate or manage goal-directed behavior.

These are described as distinct pieces of a regulatory system that can be activated, combined, or deactivated at will.

According to the EREI model, the HSC is in the early stages of this developmental process, as it has not yet developed a robust (or effective) self-regulation system. Some HSCs are better than others at managing their emotions. But even those who have very effective systems still need help to grow into more successful people who can live effectively in today's world.

The trick is for adults to help children learn how to develop these skills in childhood before they turn 18.

In many cases, it's really the adults in the child's life who need to learn how to help the child manage their emotions better. The goal is for everyone in the family to participate in efforts aimed at helping children have more of a sense of control over their environment.

The EREI model suggests that developing effective emotion regulation skills involves two basic pieces:

1. Improving self-awareness
2. Improving affect management.

Most parents and teachers are already quite good at teaching children how to identify their feelings: something like "I feel sad because you took my toy." However, this awareness isn't enough to lead children from frustration or sadness to resilience and healthy social relationships.

The EREI model proposes that developing effective emotion regulation skills requires teaching children to improve their ability to modulate their negative affect, and therefore their relationships with other people. It's not enough for children to play well with others, they must be able to manage the frustrations that come from having a friend or family member who's bad at sharing, who gets jealous or isolated from others, who tends to play up or down without regard for others' feelings.

This is where the emotional intelligence skills of self-awareness and empathy come into play. They're both abilities that HSCs can learn early in life, but which may be depleted over time as children are encouraged to avoid their own emotions and the feelings of others.

The EREI model suggests that children can learn to do both kinds of emotional regulation: self-awareness and affect management. They can learn how to be more self-aware, so they can better identify their own feelings and needs. And they can learn how to manage those feelings so that they're not overwhelming the kid or invading their own relationship with others.

This can happen if parents and teachers learn how to help HSC children use these skills for managing their own emotions and for understanding the emotions of others.

Parents and teachers may be able to provide this guidance in several ways, depending on their own ability to provide emotional support, and on the child's needs.

For example, if a child is having problems with one or more developmental milestones that interfere with their peer relationships, some special help may be needed from a family therapist or pediatrician. If the child is having difficulties with social skills at school, a behavioral approach such as reinforcement can be helpful. If the child is experiencing difficulty at home and at school, a multi-dimensional approach is probably needed. This might involve the services of an EI coach, a mental health therapist, and a behavioral specialist.

HSC children can benefit greatly from both social-behavioral programs and interventions that help them learn to recognize their own emotional states. It's also very helpful for HSC children to learn how to manage those emotions more effectively.

In one recent study, HSC children who received training in emotion regulation were more likely to develop better friendships with their peers than those who did not receive this kind of support.

A recent study on the effects of an EI program for HSCs found that participants who had received the training were better able to manage their emotions in a variety of situations. They also had improved social skills, such as increased empathy and less anxiety.

There are many other approaches to working with troubled children, including behavioral interventions, cognitive therapy, and psychodynamic therapy.

The EREI model suggests that these methods can work well when they're combined with a focus on developing a child's emotional regulation skills.

The EREI model proposes that these skills can be learned through instruction and practice. However, children with HSCs need a lot of help learning how to identify and manage the emotions that may undermine their efforts to develop healthy relationships with others. This is especially true for children who are on the autism spectrum.

In one recent study, parents who reported more stress in their parent-child relationship were less likely to give their kids help with managing their emotions. This suggests that some families need professional assistance from a counselor or coach who can help improve the parent-child relationship while also teaching emotion regulation skills.

Most of what we know about emotional intelligence comes from studies on adults, especially in the workplace.

Studies of HSC students suggest that they can benefit from programs that teach them how to improve their ability to recognize and manage their emotions. These techniques have been found to help HSC students manage emotions and improve social skills in a variety of situations, including interactions with peers, family members, and authority figures like teachers. These skills may also help HSCs be more confident and better able to handle stress.

One recent study has shown that children with high sensitivity can learn these skills at school by using education programs such as the EI program developed by Daniel Goleman and his colleagues.

Before a child is diagnosed with HSC, it's difficult to determine how much they'll benefit from an emotional regulation intervention.

One recent study has shown that children who received a cognitive-behavioral treatment for anxiety problems benefited more than other children who received similar interventions. However, this research only looked at a limited number of children with HSCs.

The results of other studies are also promising, but researchers aren't sure exactly how beneficial these methods really are in the long run.

A recent study suggests that when cognitive-behavioral therapy is combined with parenting education, the benefits may last longer than when therapy is used alone.

Some people with HSCs may have a genetic tendency towards HSCs, developing the characteristic at a very young age. Some of these children will have a normal developmental trajectory early in life and then develop the disorder as they get older.

It's also possible for an unmedicated child to go on to develop HSCs because of traumatic or challenging experiences after their diagnosis. People with HSCs may also have different characteristics that affect their ability to regulate their emotions than those without the condition.

Some people with high sensitivity are more capable of controlling emotions than others, which is one reason why researchers tend not to base emotional regulation programs solely on techniques that work for all people with HSCs.

Get the HSC to Talk to Parents, an Adult, or a Psychiatrist

If a child is not talking to you, then try an adult or a psychiatrist.

A high-sensitive child can sometimes get stuck in the mindset of not wanting to talk about anything with adults, but as they grow older, this will no longer be the case. Just because they won't tell you what's bothering them doesn't mean it isn't bothering them. So if you ever suspect that something is wrong with your high-sensitive child and they do not want to talk about it, seek help from an adult or a psychiatrist who has experience in dealing with children of the same nature. In some circumstances though where there is a real danger to life and limb then contact authorities first so that they can become involved if necessary.

After a while, the high-sensitive child will learn that they can talk to their parents about anything.

When a child is younger and not wanting to talk with adults is due to their being in a stage of development where they want to have things their way and get mad when that does not happen. The high-sensitive child is no different, and even though they might be acting out more than the average kid, it still doesn't mean that something is wrong with them or someone has done something bad for them when this happens. It is just another stage of development along with the other stages like walking, talking, potty training, and so on. So just let it go as much as you can. If an adult is involved that can be a good way to see what is wrong and get help with it, but if you know your child well enough you can just sit them down and have a talk.

If your high-sensitive child is having trouble getting along with their peers, then maybe they are not really in the right school environment for them or something else is at work. If a high-sensitive child finds himself or herself in an environment where he or she does not like the people around him or her, then yes, it can mean that he or she has something wrong with him or her.

This kind of behavior might be in contrast to what you would expect from your child if they were acting more normal and being more social. The problem is that the high-sensitive child may not be able to tell you that they are feeling sad and worried too. This is because they do not really know how to express these feelings and so hide them better than others can. So if they are having trouble getting along with others in school, then you should talk with the teacher, or if it happens at home, it should be handled by your child's parents first before talking to you about it.

People are different and so are their reactions. A high-sensitive child can make friends easily, but when things start going bad between them, then maybe this means something is wrong with them. It is possible that your child can have friends, but just not too many of them if he or she is very sensitive. People can be hurtful and so he or she might take things the wrong way and feel sad about it.

A high-sensitive child can, in fact, have a lot of friends. They might even have more than their peers do because their parents will not mind taking them places more often like playgrounds where they can play with other children. You should also get to know the parents of your high-sensitive child's friends as you will probably be going over to their homes to get your child from school or for other reasons.

If you have a high-sensitive child, it is best to treat them like any other child as much as possible. That means that they should be allowed to make their own choices and decisions. Give them your love and encouragement.

Research finds that children with the highest risk of developing a mental health disorder by age 14-20 are those who are highly sensitive and show signs of anxiety or depression. Unfortunately, they often don't speak up about their needs.

The most common causes of concern for these kids are not being able to identify what works for them in school, feeling overwhelmed by social situations, or becoming anxious when confronted with new stimuli—including voices and sounds that may be very mild but seem too loud in their head. Not being able to make sense of the noise and sensory input in school is a huge factor. They have to learn at home, but not in school when they can't cope with the noise and do "not knowing" what is causing it. In addition to academic struggles, there are other problems related to these children's sensitivity.

"If you're highly sensitive," says child psychologist Mary Ann Chapin, "you're likely also to be creative, intuitive, artistic, or spiritual—not just introverted. High sensitivity is an evolutionary trait that puts us on high alert for potential threats. If you're on the very high end of the scale, you risk being overwhelmed by your sensitivities and not functioning optimally. This will often manifest itself in difficulties with social interactions, both at home and school."

"Research shows that highly sensitive people may have depression more easily," Chapin says. "They also are more likely to have anxiety disorders. But while often a source of concern for parents, this trait is not necessarily inherently problematic. People have a tremendously wide range of sensitivities. It's what you do with it that matters."

At home, parents can help by saying, "I can see that you're upset" or "You look like you're having a hard time." This lets the child know that his parent has noticed and may be able to help. That is immensely reassuring for these children. If they don't get that reassurance, they will feel alone in dealing with their struggles, as Chapin explains:

"This is the kind of sensitivity that allows them to be easily overstimulated and annoyed by loud noises, bright lights, and strong smells—even when others might not notice," she says. "If they can't tolerate their own sensitivities, it can lead to trying to repress them or ignore them—which are never successful strategies and often lead to more severe anxiety. And if the child is very sensitive he might not be able to cope with painful realities in life or connect with those around him.

"The parent's role is not just to reassure the child," Chapin says. "The child also needs an open and honest conversation that explains what's going on for him, what's making him feel uncomfortable, and how he can do something about it."

Chapin recommends talking about sensitivity training for children under 10 years old—a time when they are still learning to control their reactions. "It's the only way for them to develop the mental and emotional skills they need to handle these feelings."

Parents can help children who are over 10 by talking about their worries. The goal is to help them understand what they're feeling and how to handle themselves more effectively. "They need to learn that it's not just about mustering up willpower or fighting against their sensitivity," she says. "They need to recognize that some feelings signal a real need for help—and then figure out what that help is."

The earlier you start talking with your child, the better, she says. That gives you a chance to build rapport and show that you're on their side. "Children who come from homes with stable parents who have a good relationship with each other are more likely to develop confidence and the ability to cope, even if their sensitivities are higher than average," Chapin says.

The research also found that the most common mental health disorders among highly sensitive kids are:

Anxiety disorder - Over 20 percent of highly sensitive children report having some form of anxiety, compared to just over 10 percent of their peers. Because these children tend to be hard on themselves, they often internalize negative events and respond with criticism or self-blame. This can lead to feelings of sadness and loneliness.

ADHD - Attention Deficit Hyperactivity Disorder - Researchers found that almost 15 percent of highly sensitive children had some form of ADHD, compared to about 7 percent of their peers.

Depression - About 4 percent of highly sensitive kids experience major depression, compared to 2 percent. Because of these intense emotions they may retreat into themselves and feel cut off from friends or family. They are also more likely to become anxious when told that their fears are crazy and other people in the world think everyone is crazy too.

Though these disorders are common among this group, it's important to note that they can be managed fairly easily with good medical care and psychotherapy—especially if children feel okay with coming out and speaking openly about what they need.

Talk to your kids about their sensitivities and offer ideas for coping.

"We know from brain research that the very sensitive person is more active in the right side of the brain, which is also where emotions are processed," Chapin says. "He or she pays more attention to detail, can be more emotionally reactive, and is often overwhelmed by stimuli. On the other hand, this same person—when aware of his or her own sensitivity—can develop greater self-control by using both sides of their brains."

In the Shadows of Our Words

I'm sometimes struck by how steadfastly children reflect their parents' mentality to life. Nearly in the same words, they utilize similar expressions. How are you and your family managing these defiling "infections?"

- Be aware of the sorts of discussions that fill your home, and be sufficiently striking to alter visitors who may be developing to a "grievances and debacles" speech.
- Watch your child's openness to the media. Regardless of whether the material isn't age-confined, sensitive children are frequently entirely powerless against upsetting symbolism. Simultaneously, regardless of how cautious you are, your child will be presented with some shocking certainties about their reality. Papers, magazines, TV, and classmates are altogether proficient transporters of upsetting information. On the off chance that they experience something that is disturbing them, set aside the effort to hear their considerations and feelings. Ensure that they have an age-proper handle of what occurred. At the point when I converse with a confused child, I give exceptional consideration to their daydreams and questions, because these give me a thought of the profundity of their agreement and the sort of criticism they need. By allowing them inquiries to control the discussion, I rapidly find the things that are upsetting them, thus I realize how best to help and console them.
- Stay inside the domain of your child's inquiries and answer these deferentially. You'll see that they can utilize you as an encouraging reference point. On the off chance that something is upsetting your child, what would it be advisable for them to do about it? Is there an age-fitting reaction that they can make? Is this the ideal opportunity for them to gather little change from the family to make a gift to a good cause, help cook a feast, or say a prayer?
- Partners do fight. Indeed, research shows two or three arguments don't imply that a marriage is unhealthy. Yet, obviously, there are valuable and ruinous methods of belligerence. Allow your children to become familiar with the abilities of aware contradiction from you.

- Allow them to perceive how well you hear each out other, how you can come to viable tradeoffs, and, obviously, how you're ready to experience the cycle of the statement of regret and pardoning when one of you has "blown it."
- Your child needn't bother with you to be genuinely projectile evidence. If you are experiencing a troublesome time, continue to identify with him. Consider telling him something about the difficulties you are confronting, how you are feeling, and what you intend to improve. Tell him how he can deal with helping you. In some cases, this can be just as basic as "If it's not too much trouble, continue to put forth an attempt at school." A child benefits by having a real reason when there is a resistive home.
- Own your feelings of fear. If you are criticized as being something of a "worry pot" at that point, rather than allowing your feelings of trepidation to gush out over into your child, concede this weakness to your child. Help them with seeing that they don't really have to feel the things that you feel.

Appreciation

The way that our children catch our regular discussions additionally gives us some awesome open doors. Envision your child's experience as they catch your accounts of appreciation and fervor. Envision them catching discussions about your victories and wins at work: how you at last fastened down the serious deal, or about the brilliant recommendation you got from a customer. How frequently do we talk about the many things we must be grateful for?

Studies have connected appreciation to feelings of satisfaction (Walker and Pitts, 1998), joy, pride, and expectation (Overwalle, Mervielde, and De Schuyter, 1995). In a genuinely late Gallup (1998) study of American teens, more than 90% said that offering thanks helped them with feeling cheerful. Emmons and Crumpler (2000) have discovered that a cognizant spotlight on appreciation makes life seriously satisfying, important, and beneficial. Appreciation associates us with other people; it cradles us against jealousy and encourages us to take an interest in the master plan.

Appreciation encourages us to process frustrations and losses and to make the most of our triumphs (Emmons and Shelton, 2002).

I would say, sensitive children who have built up a feeling of appreciation are simpler to help. They are better ready to take responsibility for challenges and they are more co-employable with their parents. They appear to be much more like themselves.

- I believe that sensitive children can retain the direction of appreciation through basic, ordinary collaborations with their parents. Regardless of whether you're driving the vehicle, or getting your child into bed, pay special attention to liberties to show appreciation.

- Presumably, it's a smart idea to teach our children the propensity for saying "thank you so much" in their initial years. However, remember that children presumably just begin to comprehend the standards of appreciation by about the age of nine (Gleason and Weintraub, 1976). In this way, younger sensitive children, step-by-step raise their mindfulness with huge spots of affection and adaptability.

- As your children get more established, let them comprehend that "thank-you" isn't just about decorum. It's a method of perceiving that they are cherished and that they can love.

- Notice thoughtful gestures in your child and say thanks to him for these deeds.

- Work on showing appreciation in your own life. Many individuals have discovered that this works best when it's set up as a component of their everyday schedules. Consider recording the things for which you are appreciative.

•   Appreciation will in general be tied in with "assessing the situation." So don't anticipate that your sensitive child should remember they are good fortune when they're furious. Hang tight for more quiet waters before reminding your child to think about some of the superb facts in her day-to-day existence.

•   Show your children to see the imperceptible. Urge them to recognize parts of themselves that they regularly ignore.

•   Keep your statement! Understanding what you will do, and when, regularly has a major effect on sensitive children. Any fundamental hurt, disappointment, or question will decrease your capacity to converse with your child about appreciation.

•   In age and capacity suitable ways, give your children freedoms to help you, and say thanks to them for their endeavors.

CHAPTER 8:

HSC ages 14 to 20. Teens

How to Handle a Highly Sensitive Adolescent

Teenagers are a tough breed to deal with. It can be difficult for parents to know how best to help their teenage children navigate the turbulent years of adolescence and prepare for adulthood.

Whether your teenager is showing signs of anger, self-harming behavior, or acting out behaviors like truancy—these are high-stress times, and taking care of yourself is crucial! We'll show you how to take care of yourself while also teaching your teen the skills needed for adulthood.

Challenge Perceptions

Because they are intelligent and self-removed doesn't imply that they are always right. They may contemplate something they learned in school or they might be pestered by a film they saw and structure an assessment on it. Yet, it doesn't naturally imply that their conclusions are adjusted or even right. They are children and they are as yet during the time spent framing their own feelings, noticing adults, and figuring out their reality. HSCs have the upside of being more thoughtful than their partners.

Be that as it may, they may frequently put together their judgment and sentiments concerning their own viewpoint. In that capacity, the data they hold might be fragmented or even defective.

To help them with this, empower your highly sensitive kid to develop their point of view. Try not to reveal to them through and through that they are incorrect.

Reveal to them that they can think about an alternate assessment or even a contrary one.

What Is a Highly Sensitive Teen?

HSC stands for Highly Sensitive Child. About one in five people are HSC. It is an innate trait based on differences in the neurological system. Young children, particularly preschoolers and toddlers are HSC. If you have a social, happy, outgoing child, they can be HSC too! The important thing is to support your child's natural temperament and help them learn healthy self-regulation skills.

There are two kinds of sensitive people: The highly sensitive child and someone with 'low sensory processing sensitivity.' They can both act as introverts or extroverts. They feel the same way about things but differently on the outside—for example, activity level or how outgoing they are.

The person with 'low sensory sensitivity' is less likely to show sensitive signs such as hypersensitivity to noise. They are less likely to show other signs of HSC, but they can still act like an HSC, and need support too!

How Do I Know If My Child Is a Highly Sensitive Teen?

Showing some signs is not enough. Your teenager should be open about their sensitive nature and ask for help! It's important to monitor your teenager's reactions. You'll need to monitor how often they cry at the drop of a hat, are overly emotional, and have difficulty communicating with others. They might have trouble getting along with others or having non-verbal communication.

They might be too sensitive to sounds and touch. They might find it hard to show their feelings, have a difficult time in social situations, or find it hard to make new friends.

And while being an HSC isn't a bad thing, they can have difficulties doing things that others may not have thought about. For example, hiding things from others, or frequently needing alone time. As adults, they may struggle with physical and emotional health issues that are linked to the brain's malleability during adolescence because of their high sensitivity. They may experience depression, anxiety, or have difficulty making decisions. They can pick up on and be affected by other people's anxiety and stress in a way that others don't, which can make them uncomfortable and cause them to feel stressed too.

HSCs are often labeled as being overwhelmed, and it is important to talk to your teenager about this.

How Can I Help My HSC?

- Firstly, understand that they won't want to ask for help even if they're feeling overwhelmed. This is because sensitive children don't want their needs met any more than anyone else does. They want to be able to do things themselves and not talk about their emotions.
- Let your teenager know you want them to be able to take care of themselves. The more mature this is, the greater support they will have for managing their own life. Offer assistance if they ask for it, but don't overdo it. Help them set goals and make plans, but don't micromanage them or tell them what to do. Your teenager can feel like you are controlling what they do and that can cause problems later on in life.
- When they can't handle something, just make sure they know it's okay to not be okay. If they are struggling, you can ask them what else you can do to help them. You can encourage them to set aside time for self-care and stress management.

Take a little time each day to talk about what is going on in their life. Be mindful of their reactions and try not to overdo it, but also be mindful of your own reactions so you don't add too much stress to your teenager's life by getting angry or upset.
- Letting them know that you respect their sensitivity is helpful. They will be more likely to ask for help and less likely to mask their sensitive nature because of shame or embarrassment.
- Teenagers with a highly sensitive nature need their space. They know they are different, and it will be helpful to let them know that you understand their difference and that it is okay. But don't let your teenager think they can shrug off problems or not try to solve them. It's important to encourage them to take responsibility for their behavior and work towards making positive changes in their life.
- Asking other people who are HSC what worked for them as a teenager can be helpful too. However, you mustn't compare your teenager to other kids because no two people are alike.
- Tell your teenager who they are and what makes them unique. This is especially important if they are having difficulties because people may not understand that their behavior isn't a sign of laziness or lack of personal responsibility.
- Help your teenager understand their sensitivity. They will be more likely to seek help if they know that other people know too and that you want them to do well in life. You can point out how being HSC can help them in some ways such as having better mental health, increased awareness and perception, and better social skills.
- Take time to listen to your teenager even when it's hard sometimes. They will learn from this about the power of communication with others which will be helpful for everyone later in life.

What Does the Future Hold For My HSC?

As your teenager grows up, they will need to learn the skills needed to manage their sensitivity. These skills include being less sensitive and better-controlling emotions.

- Help your teenager develop their social skills. Work with them in activities that help them to practice giving and receiving feedback from others. If your teenager is shy, encourage them to take small steps towards interacting with people. This could include starting conversations with strangers or making friends at school (it can be hard for HSCs to make friends).
- Encourage your teen to go out and get involved in groups/activities where they can meet new people and make more friends at school/work. Your teenager may be too shy to start such activities on their own, so it will be helpful if you can help them.
- Encourage your teenager to try new things. Not only is this good for stretching themselves and learning about new experiences, but it can also help them to meet new people who may become friends. Your teenager mustn't let their sensitivity stand in the way of doing things they don't want to do or not trying new things because they have a low tolerance for pain or negative emotions like anxiety. In fact, if their social development is behind other kids, they are likely to feel isolated and even more sensitive as a result of this.
- Encourage them to think about what they can do to make themselves less sensitive. Lots of things can be done such as working out or exercising, getting a new hobby, learning how to play a musical instrument or reading books. HSCs may also want to think about asking their parents for help with this so that they can learn more about controlling their emotions.
- Help your teenager understand that they are not lazy or sad or any other negative labels the world may place on them because of their sensitivity. Letting everyone know that you don't expect them to be able to do things like everyone else does is a

good thing because it lets them know that they are valued for how they are and not just for something they lack. There is a lot to consider as your teenager reaches adolescence, and it's important to use your sensitivity both as a positive and negative in these years. Teach them how to be independent and help them to understand that they don't have to live up to other people's expectations of what their life should look like because they have unique qualities that will serve them well in the future. It's important for parents of HSCs that you both know how you feel about yourself so that you can give your teenager the same message.

- Finally, HSCs are known for their focus and determination, so make sure you take this time as an opportunity for your teenager to get started on what will likely become a fulfilling career later in life. You've already taught them empathy, sensitivity, and compassion; make sure you help them learn how to channel these traits into something that will serve them well in the future. Doing things with your teenager is important but it's also just as important to give them time on their own. Make sure they have some quiet time each day so they can reflect and find a way to work out the frustrations of what happens in school from day to day. Take this time as an opportunity to teach your child that emotions are a normal part of life and that they shouldn't be ashamed for having certain ones.

Accept the Adolescent's Need to Distance Themselves From Their Parents

At some point in their adolescent years, children will want to distance themselves—or push away—from their parents. This can be a source of pain and confusion for both the child and the parent, but there is actually a reason behind this behavior. The adolescent is trying to establish individuality by separating from his/her parents. This is an important stage of development that may only last for a few weeks or months. It's also important to remember that just because your young person has distanced himself/herself from you doesn't mean they don't love or need you as much as before. Much of their need to distance themselves is a result of confusion and fear. That led to this question from the reader:

"How Can I Know If My Adolescent Child Is In denial About Issues That Are Difficult for Him?"

"He appears to be distant from me but he isn't avoiding me. I am supportive of our relationship and have no reason to believe that it would be better if he felt more comfortable being more independent. He does not verbally ask for or expresses anything just know what? "

"I Feel Like He Knows And Is Not Sharing With Me. What Should I Do?"

This parent is concerned that her teenage son is avoiding talking to her about something. Could he be in denial? What can she do to encourage him to open up and talk about what's on his mind?

The following information provides answers for this parenting dilemma. When a child distances himself or herself from the parent, it can make them feel unsure of how to respond, and that leaves you feeling a bit lost and confused.

You need to remember that your adolescent child really does love you and needs you but at the same time, he/she wants more space than they used to have when they were younger. Depending on how the two of you interact with each other will determine to a large extent how quickly this process of distancing takes place.

A parent's response to their child's desire for more distance will have a lot to do with at what point in the separation/individuation process the child is in. The separation/individuation process occurs when an adolescent moves away from his/her parents and family to become more independent and unique. As part of this process, he or she will want to separate from the family unit and establish his or her own identity, as well as create a healthier relationship with both parents (authority figures). There may be times when your child wants more time alone and becomes secretive about his whereabouts. The less you interfere, the faster he will move through this stage of separation.

This is a normal phase in your child's development and it should occur sometime between the ages of five through 12 (average age 11). The important thing to remember is that it will not last forever and that your child does love you and needs you. It's perfectly normal for an adolescent to want to distance from their parents at some point during adolescence. Your job is to encourage and support this effort without interfering or helping too much. You also need to respect his new boundaries by staying out of his room when he requests privacy, respecting his time alone with friends, etc.

This is a time when your child is trying to get a better handle on what makes him who he is—both as a person and as an individual. He will want more privacy and to be able to spend more time with his friends, which can put you in a bit of a bind. Although it may not seem like it at the time, this stage of development is critical for your child's future development. It's during this stage that he will make important decisions about his career path, his values, as well as relationships with other people (family, friends, and peers).

As part of the separation/individuation process, the adolescent also needs you to accept and respect their desire for more privacy than when they were younger. They are trying to separate from you and establish their own identity—and independence—so it's also important for you not to interfere or get in the way of their efforts.

As the parent, you can provide limited amounts of assistance if they ask for it. Just make sure to help them if they tell you they want your assistance. It can be very helpful and reassuring for your adolescent child to know that you are there for him/her but that is a different situation than when they are asking for (and receiving) a lot of help. Letting him/her know that you will be there for them if they need you is helpful but not necessary to make this separation/individuation process occur.

This process usually occurs over some time during the teenage years. It can take several years before an adolescent reaches adulthood and should have a lot more independence and proper boundaries in place, but your child needs to go through this process and to experience these feelings of separation as part of becoming an independent adult. For parents, it can be challenging to see how quickly their children grow up, get older and move away from them. That doesn't mean it won't come as a happy surprise when your adolescent child finally does leave home.

While this is a normal phase in your child's development for the separation/individuation process, it can be challenging to see it in action. Many parents feel confused and are wondering why their adolescent child seems so distant and not talking about what he's thinking or feeling. There can be a lot of confusion and uncertainty as to whether or not your child is finally moving forward with his/her separation from you. The first step for you to take when your adolescent child becomes more distant from you is to communicate openly and honestly about this development with them. Your words may be received as frustration, anger, disappointment, etc., but they are important. If you start to talk with them about your feelings, it can help them better understand where you are coming from and will allow you to bond more closely. It can be good for both of you as well as a way for your child to learn some important life lessons during his/her adolescent years.

This is a difficult stage of development for many parents but it's important that you let your child know about your feelings and that you're available to talk if they want. If they don't, the separation/individuation process will still occur on its own timetable.

Regardless of their age or stage in development, children are always going to have questions about who they are and where they fit into the overall scheme of things. You must listen to what your child has to say, hear his/her perspective, and accept him/her where he/she is at this point in time. Your child will love you and admire you all the more for treating him/her with love, respect and dignity during this period.

Unfortunately, separation (or the lack thereof) does not necessarily mean that children have a lot of problems at home or are having difficulty interacting with their parents. They may be getting along just fine at home but still feeling insecure about themselves and their ability to create their own identity. To make matters worse, they may not feel as if they are ready to leave or need more time to separate from you. They may feel like they have to go through some more steps before they're ready to move out and form their own identity.

It's not unusual for children to act out as a way of showing their feelings. This tends to happen more commonly in girls than in boys. If this is the case, you may notice your child hanging around with a particular group of young people, spending less time with her/his family, and be less responsive when you call or ask her/him if she/he wants to spend the day with you or have dinner with the family. If a parent is not aware of these feelings, it may be interpreted as rejection by the parent.

In boys, there's no evidence that an inability or unwillingness to separate leads to aggression. But in girls, parents who do not allow their daughters to separate and develop their own identity are at risk for having a daughter who is filled with repressed anger and withdrawn from her parents. This insecure girl may unconsciously act out her anger (more often toward her mother than father), resulting in acting out behavior such as moodiness and saying hurtful things. At this stage of development, if she doesn't have a strong sense of self, she may develop eating problems or become overly concerned with how she looks.

Help in Coping With High School

If you have a highly sensitive child you know they need more than just the average person. They'll be more sensitive to smells, textures, noise, and light and may often have a very hard time developing social connections with peers because they simply don't understand why others can't seem to read their minds.

They also have trouble regulating their emotions which can lead to out-of-control temper tantrums or deep depression. And they may get overwhelmed really easily so try not to go from zero to 100 in one second with them.

Believe me, when I say this, you are a parent of a highly sensitive child you are already doing an amazing job and you can do even better with these tips!

- When your child is going through a major teen period you need to be prepared for this and teach your child how to best deal with it. There may be many things that can stress them out such as the newness of high school, hormones, peer pressure, Facebook, having to make decisions and so many other things that unfortunately are part of growing up.
- If you have a highly sensitive child help them find ways to manage their feelings instead of reacting in an out of control manner which can lead to acting out or even self-harming. Make sure they know what they are feeling and why they are feeling it before getting angry about it. Involving a counselor may be something you want to do if your child has really deep feelings about their situation.
- Creating a routine that works for your child will help them feel calm and prepared for what is going to happen and build that healthy self-esteem that they need so much. This way when they begin feeling overwhelmed and unfocused as they are going through these changes in their life it will help them gain

back control. And when a crisis does happen as the loss of a parent or something else really bad you can be there to help them deal with it. Small changes like this can really make a big difference in your child's life.

- Your highly sensitive child needs to know they can come to you with their feelings and you will love them no matter what. So hug them when they need it, send them a text letting them know how much you love them and that you are there for them no matter what. Remind them that the world is full of beauty but just because they are highly sensitive doesn't mean that there is something wrong with them or that they need to be scared of everything out in the world.
- It is very important to include your highly sensitive child in family activities and have fun with them. To give them a sense of security and love. As an HSC you are going to need your family around you as much as possible so make sure they know that this is ok, especially with the teen years being so intense. You want your child to know that family is good and the bond between each other will help them get through the tough times easier.

All of these things are important and if everyone takes the time to do just a few of these things it will make a big difference in your child's life. So don't wait, start building that sense of emotional confidence as soon as you can. You will be glad you did.

Sexuality for an HSC

Sexuality can be difficult for anyone, but it can be especially challenging for highly sensitive children. Their moods are often ruled by their perceptions and even the slightest input of information from the environment. Sexuality is not just about sexual activities, it is a part of an individual's personality, identity, and well-being. It is important to explore sexuality with highly sensitive children to help them develop a healthy emotional attachment to themselves and others.

- Think of your child's sensitivity as an asset. Allow them to live in a world that does not expect them to always overcompensate or "toughen up." Allowing your child time and space will allow him time and space to explore sexuality without any pressure. Sexuality is an important part of being human, and most people learn about it at a young age.
- A problem with sexuality for highly sensitive children may be unrealistic expectations from others, and the inability to feel that one's needs are valid. Encourage your child to accept that he may not be able to meet other people's sexual expectations. He will have to find happiness in his own way.
- One of the best predictors of a highly sensitive child being able to form healthy relationships with others is having an understanding and accepting parent (or an accepting adult). If a child feels that their needs are not being met by you, he will likely be unwilling and/or unable to communicate his feelings.
- Children of high sensitive parents often undervalue or dismiss their own feelings. They may feel viewed as the problem, rather than the solution. Helping them identify and understand their emotions will help them become more responsible adults who can empathize with others.
- There are many challenges in raising a highly sensitive child, but it is definitely worth giving your best effort. Remember that your child is an individual with his own unique strengths and weaknesses—do not compare him to other children and try to get him to change his personality into being "more normal." Allow him to be who he is, and seek out opportunities for him to build his self-esteem in a safe environment.

Be patient with yourself, your partner, and your highly sensitive child.

Nurturing the 'Gift' of Sensitivity

"The Child's Gift: Sensitivity" by Elaine Aron Ph.D., HSC author, and expert reveals that at least one-quarter of us are born highly sensitive people. This is good news because it means that more of us are born with the innate ability to make a positive contribution, to be able to see 'unseen dangers,' and to be able to raise issues before they become major problems. However, even more of us may be born with this ability, and those who are highly sensitive often don't realize that they have these gifts.

Healthy Communication

The necessity of communication in everyday life is an often-overlooked keystone to success and happiness. The nuances of healthy communication are as unique as the people who practice it. By referring to this study, it will help high-sensitivity teens learn how healthy communication can strengthen their relationships with others and find their place in this world with less strain on their emotions.

One of the most important aspects that high sensitivity teens must learn about before entering adulthood is how to communicate effectively. This skill can affect their relationships within the school, at home, and in the workplace. Also, it will help them to make more assertive decisions in times of stress and have a positive impact on their self-esteem. Communication is a two-way street, so like with any other skill it takes practice to master.

According to Elaine Aron (2012), sensitive people are those who have an innate ability to sense what others are feeling as well as an exceptional ability to feel their own feelings. They suffer from intense emotions and feel "overloaded" in highly stimulating environments. However, they are also highly empathic and caring toward others. Often, this trait shows up early in childhood and continues into adulthood.

High sensitivity is a fairly new term in the psychological community. In fact, Elaine Aron (2012) was the first to describe this sensitivity as a personality trait in 1991. Before that time, "sensitive" was used as a negative word. We now have a better understanding of this trait as it has been found that highly sensitive children make up 20% of the population (Aron 2012). Their high levels of empathy allow them to have keen insight into other people's feelings and quickly develop strong bonds with those around them. As they grow older, those bonds are tested by many of the challenges they face, specifically in their ability to communicate effectively.

Communication is a two-way street. The communication process starts with an emitter who is sending information to the receiver who in return will send a message back to the emitter through either verbal or nonverbal channels (Watkins 2012). However, because sensitive people are so focused on other's feelings and emotions, they often overlook their own communication needs which leads to problems in relationships.

High sensitivity teens have difficulty understanding how other people feel during conversations because of their self-focused nature (Aron 2012). They need to learn that other people have their own agenda, not just their feelings. This will help them focus on the other person and tune into their body language, instead of their own beliefs and feelings.

As sensitive teens develop into adults, they must learn to manage the intensity of their emotions as well as the feelings of others. Self-awareness is crucial when it comes to effective communication (Aron 2012). For example, if one person is feeling over-sensitive and emotional during a conversation then they might need some time for themselves before continuing. This can be a hard concept for sensitive people to learn because they are often concerned about other people's feelings and they have trouble being direct and honest. This struggle to handle negative emotions can strain sensitive people's relationships with those around them. However, sensitive teens must learn how to communicate effectively with others so they don't suffer from social isolation.

Due to the overstimulation that sensitive people feel in large groups, they usually like one-on-one conversations because it allows them the chance to focus on the feelings of another person without being bombarded by their own emotions (Aron 2012). This helps them to become more self-aware and develop their own unique style of communication.

For sensitive people, sometimes it can be difficult to determine who is talking among a group of people because any interaction with another person will cause them to feel immediately connected and understood. Therefore, they must learn to listen for meaning and be open-minded when someone is sharing an opinion or their feelings. It's not always easy for sensitive people to do this because they tend to overanalyze others' words, so they must practice listening more than talking during conversations.

Of all the things that may occur during a conversation, the one that makes the most impact on sensitive teens is body language (Watkins 2012). If the body language of the person they are with is closed, then they typically feel uncomfortable and will try to change the subject or walk away. In contrast, if the body language is open, then they will continue to communicate effectively. The ability to read body language effectively can help sensitive teens understand what other people are feeling and allow them to build deeper relationships with those around them.

During a conversation, sensitive teens must also learn how to pick up on vocal cues. It's common for them to act impulsively during a conversation because of their heightened sensitivity towards their own feelings (Holliday & Palmer 2011). This often causes them to blurt out things that could be perceived as inappropriate or rude. On the other hand, if a sensitive teen is trying to express their feelings, then they tend to exaggerate their voice and use too many words (Holliday & Palmer 2011). As a result, sensitive people may be misinterpreted or misunderstood by the people they are speaking with.

Sensitive teens must learn how to hear what others are saying without any emotion attached. This means putting aside their own thoughts and beliefs as well as becoming less self-focused so they can focus on the conversation instead of on themselves. Sensitive teens must also think about how other people feel when communicating because they will often consider others' feelings while listening.

When it comes to communicating, sensitive teens need to practice listening more than talking to receive the necessary information during a conversation (Aron 2012). Their desire to get their thoughts across can be overwhelming and can cause them to take on inappropriate behavior as a means of expressing themselves. In contrast, if they can listen without interrupting or speaking first then they will be able to receive and interpret the other person's messages.

Why HSCs Benefit from Social Media Detoxes

When your child is struggling with social media, it can be difficult to know how to help. It's easy for anything on the internet to feel dangerous, and when your child begins cutting down on their social media usage it can feel like you're taking away a vital part of their identity. However, there are many benefits associated with social media detoxes—and these benefits extend beyond just your child's well-being. If you're looking for ways that might help reverse or at least improve symptoms related to your family member's struggles with mental health issues such as anxiety and depression, then these resources are a great place to start.

As you search for apps and websites that can help you regulate the time your child spends online, here are a few benefits to consider.

Increased Self-Awareness

One of the most important challenges associated with social media detoxes is getting people to realize exactly how much time they're spending online. When your child first begins limiting their social media usage it can feel like they're being deprived of something vital, but the reality is that limiting the time they spend on social media is likely to improve their quality of life and make it easier for them to function in real-life situations that have nothing to do with technology.

Improved Focus

When your child spends too much time on social media, they don't get enough time to read books or do their homework. Too much time online makes it harder for the child to focus on their work. This can be frustrating and distracting and can make it difficult for students to get their homework done promptly. Although your child may try to downplay how much time they spend on social media when they're first cutting down, the reality is that social media detoxes are likely to improve their academic performance and their ability to focus at work or school.

Improved Self-Esteem

Social media is a great place to share pictures of our accomplishments—but it can also make us feel worse about ourselves. Unfortunately, social media is a place where people feel the need to compare themselves to others and post pictures of their best moments (which can make anyone feel inadequate). When your child first begins cutting down on their social media usage, they may try to reassure you that they aren't doing it because they're unhappy with themselves. However, most people who are struggling with mental health issues will likely benefit from putting less emphasis on themselves online and more emphasis on improving the quality of their real-life relationships.

Increased Sense of Self-Control

On social media, there's a sense of urgency to everything, making it feel like people have less control over their lives than they actually do. But when your child first begins coming out of their social media comfort zone they may feel as though they're suffering through some kind of online purgatory. By forcing them to cut down on social media completely, you can help them gain control of their lives again and stop putting so much pressure on themselves.

Improved Creativity

Social media makes it easy for us to share what we're doing with the world at any given moment, but this can make it feel like we don't have any creative control over our lives or our future goals. When your child first begins coming out of their social media comfort zone, they may feel compelled to share their new-found creativity with others. However, the best thing for them to do is wait until they've actually created something worthwhile before posting it online. Not only can taking a break from social media help them develop their creativity, but it can also help them focus on more important things in their lives and stop worrying so much about what other people think.

More Time for Exercise, Reading, and Personal Hobbies

Instead of spending hours scrolling through social media all day long, your child will have plenty of extra time to do the things that they love. They will have plenty of time to exercise, take long walks in parks or go running through the countryside. They'll also have plenty of time to read many books and watch many movies. The extra time they spend doing these things will make them happier and more productive members of society and help them develop a deeper love for the world around them.

They'll Increase Their Vocabulary

Speaking of words, teens who read also get to learn new ones and thus expand their vocabulary. The more they read the more words they'll learn and the easier it will be for them to converse with sophisticated people in the future. Not only that, but if they take on a new hobby, such as learning a language, the more books they read about it the more quickly they'll be able to master it.

They'll Get Out of Their Comfort Zone

Every time a teen picks up a book he or she is getting out of their comfort zone. In fact, moving out of their comfort zone is the best way to ensure that they'll be able to learn something new and useful in the future.

In conclusion, social media is a never-ending rabbit hole that can easily get your child caught up for hours at a time on their smartphone, tablet, or computer screen. Once there, it can be extremely easy to forget about their studies or important adult responsibilities until they're in big trouble when it's almost too late. But by taking steps to help your family member learn how to manage their time online, you can make it easier for them to reach their goals and start taking care of themselves. The most important thing any parent can do is make sure that they're monitoring their child's online activity and setting healthy limitations on how much time they spend on social media. Of course, there are always exceptions to every rule—but in general, the less time your child spends on social media, the better things will be for them in the long run.

Dealing with Anxiety as an HSC

An HSC who lacks insight into their special trait might assume that they are just a jittery, anxious person destined to live a life of worry. Fortunately, it doesn't have to be this way. As you've made your way through this book, you will have come to appreciate why an HSC can easily feel overwhelmed and anxious. In fact, it's almost inevitable—being caught in a tsunami of emotions and energy fields naturally has a significant impact on a person's wellbeing. The good news is that when self-awareness and self-management skills develop, you don't have to suffer from chronic anxiety.

The Difference Between High Sensitivity & Anxiety

To the untrained eye, high sensitivity and anxiety disorders appear similar. In fact, many people use the words "sensitive" and "anxious" interchangeably. For example, someone with a phobia of small spaces will have panic attacks whenever they have to spend time in a large crowd. Their symptoms—feeling overwhelmed, shaky, jittery, and physically unwell—are the same as those reported by HSCs when they are highly stimulated.

Although not all people with anxiety disorders are HSCs and not all HSCs have anxiety disorders, there is a link between anxiety and sensitivity. HSCs tend to have particularly sensitive startle reflexes, which make them more prone to heightened emotional arousal. An individual's reflexes are determined by their genetics, which partially explains why HSCs typically report that sensitivity seems to run in their family.

Just to make matters worse, the average HSC has a vivid imagination that can fuel their anxieties even further. This is a downside of creativity! They are all too capable of imagining worst-case scenarios, which further feeds into their anxiety or panic. For example, if they feel especially shaken in a noisy environment, they may start to wonder whether they are having a heart attack and even begin to worry about how their family or friends will deal with the news of their death! This may sound melodramatic or ridiculous to a non-HSC, but the distress people with this trait feel is real.

The key difference, of course, is that non-HSCs with anxiety disorders can approach their anxiety as a mental illness that can be eliminated with the right treatment. On the other hand, an HSC will never fully eliminate their sensitivity and susceptibility to anxiety and panic.

Tips for Anxious HSCs

Ride the Wave of Anxiety—Don't Try to Fight It

Therapist Linda Walter, who specializes in working with anxious people, recommends the R.I.D.E. technique. It's a simple acronym that can help handle even the roughest of panic attacks!

- Recognize: Acknowledge that you are having a panic attack.

- Involve: Choose to engage with your surroundings. Use grounding and breathing exercises to keep yourself rooted in the present.

- Distract: This step is self-explanatory. All you need to do is find something that holds your attention, even if it's just for a few moments.

- End: Trust that even the scariest of panic attacks usually pass within a few minutes, and almost all attacks end within 30 minutes.

It may not feel like it, but anxiety can't kill you. You have the strength to make it through to the other side!

Now I will turn directly to your highly sensitive child with some advice on how to manage the possible moments of anxiety that it is normal to come in some moments of adolescence.

A mantra is another useful tool. Come up with a phrase or saying in advance and repeat it to yourself during difficult times. For instance, you could tell yourself, "This will pass," or "I just need to wait." Write it on a card and keep it in your purse or wallet so you have it on hand. You could even make it your phone wallpaper!

Master Breathing Exercises

Breathing exercises can make you feel better during times of high anxiety. Practice slow, deep breathing when you are calm until it becomes second nature. You will then be able to use this technique when anxiety strikes. To calm yourself down, begin by inhaling through your nose. Picture the air filling your lungs. Hold your breath while counting to three. Purse your lips and exhale slowly. As you breathe out, make a conscious effort to relax your body. Pay particular attention to your neck, shoulders, stomach, and jaw.

A variation of this exercise is the "Calming Counts" technique. Find a comfortable place if possible and sit down. Begin by inhaling slowly and deeply. As you exhale, tell yourself to relax. Next, take ten normal breaths. Shut your eyes and keep them closed as you count down, either in your head or out loud. You can also ask someone else to count for you if you feel very worried and unable to concentrate. As you do this exercise, make a conscious effort to relax the muscles in your body.

Watch for Patterns

Some people find that their feelings of worry and panic appear to come and go at random, but there are usually some underlying triggers. Pay close attention to the events preceding your periods of anxiety and panic.

Remember that if you are generally stressed and anxious, it won't take much to tip you over the edge into a panic attack or a state of emotional overwhelm. To thrive as an HSC, you will benefit from getting into healthy habits, such as regular meditation to manage stress.

Find a Sympathetic Mental Health Professional

If your feelings of anxiety are causing you a lot of distress, or you are having problems functioning at home, you should consider seeking professional help. However, you must choose a doctor or therapist who appreciates that some people are simply more sensitive than others, and therefore have different needs. You may need to take anti-anxiety medication if your symptoms are severe, but it's usually more effective to take a long-term approach and learn to manage your feelings.

For example, a non-HSC who has developed an anxiety disorder following a difficult period in their life can reasonably expect to make a full recovery and return to their usual low levels of anxiety, but an HSC should not be encouraged to change their personality just to fit in with society's idea of "normal."

When attending an initial consultation, ask whether they are accustomed to working with HSCs. If they aren't familiar with the term you could even bring some literature on high sensitivity with you. A caring, open-minded health professional should be willing to listen. If not, find someone else who is more on your wavelength.

Erikson's Theories

When we are aware of how the human develops then we can guide our children highly sensitive in growing well in each stage. To understand all this, Erikson and his studies come to our aid.

Erik Erikson, a formidable psychologist, developed a theory on the psychosocial development of humans from birth to adulthood.

Erikson admired Sigmund Freud and tried to build on his psychosexual stages of development. But Freud only limited his analysis of psychosocial factors in the childhood stages. For Freud, what happened to you in childhood affects and determines your adulthood. But for Erikson, he extended his analysis to adulthood, wherein development proceeds and is challenged at every stage. Though the goal of Erikson's psychosocial development theory is to help individuals realize their own struggles and understand how they can overcome specific tensions in their lives, we can also use it in terms of parenthood. When we are aware of how the human develops, according to Erikson, then we can guide our children in growing well in each stage.

According to Erik Erikson, humans develop sequentially, that is, following a specific course of actions. Humans follow a certain developmental path occurring in stages. These stages cover a certain age group, from birth to adulthood. For him, humans are not just determined by biological factors which include our genetic make-up, what we consume, or what illnesses affect us. Erikson sees humans as influenced by biological, social, and psychological factors. This is a dynamic view of the human person because it allows us to go beyond biological determination and gives us a wider perspective in understanding the human person. How we think, how we feel, what excites us, what frightens us, and what moves us to do a particular action are all influenced by many factors. When we understand how humans move forward or backward or stay in a particular stage, then we can correlate that to how they are behaving now and what their future behaviors will be. Thus, Erikson's theory is expansive and holistic, covering the entire lifetime of people.

Stages

Erikson identified eight stages of psychosocial development. Though Erikson assigns a particular age group to each stage, these ages are not rigidly fixed. For example, stage 1 is for infants, but the person can remain in such a stage for one, two, or more years depending on their environment or health. We develop sequentially, that is, from stage 1 to stage 2, and so on. We can be delayed in a particular stage, or we can be in different stages all at once depending on whether we meet the particular demands at each stage. For this book, we will simply focus on infancy to adolescence. Our role as parents are crucial in these stages and we should focus on understanding these to guide our children.

Childhood Stage:

- Stage 1: Infancy (0 to 18 months)
- Stage 2: Early Childhood (1.5 to 3 years)
- Stage 3: Play Age (3 to 5 years)
- Stage 4: School Age (5 to 12 years)

Adolescence Stage:

- Stage 5: Adolescence (12 to 18 years)

Adulthood Stage:

- Stage 6: Young Adulthood (18 to 40 years)
- Stage 7: Middle Adulthood (40 to 65 years)
- Stage 8: Maturity (65+ years)

Psychosocial Tensions

Each stage is accompanied by a particular psychosocial tension. These are decision points for the individual, the central question that predominates in each stage. There are two opposing psychological tendencies for each stage. On one hand, is the positive or constructive value and the other is the negative or dysfunctional value that an individual can imbibe. Here are the stages again with the accompanying psychosocial tensions.

- Infancy: Trust vs. Mistrust
- Early Childhood: Autonomy vs. Shame

- Play Age: Initiative vs. Guilt
- School Age: Industry vs. Inferiority
- Adolescence: Identity vs. Identity Confusion
- Young Adulthood: Intimacy vs. Isolation
- Adulthood: Generativity vs. Stagnation
- Old Age: Integrity vs. Despair

An individual must be able to resolve the particular tension in the stage where they are at. The goal is to achieve the positive value and to veer away from the dysfunctional value. The choice to achieve the positive is effortful. For children, they must have an enabling environment for them to be able to choose a constructive value. That is why our role as parents is crucial in the childhood and adolescence stages. But as people mature, they must make an effort by themselves to achieve these values. Not choosing to be trusting, for example, is tantamount to regressing to the negative value. Therefore, these psychosocial tensions are effortful for both the individual and their caretakers.

How people progress to the next stages is also dependent on the resolution of the psychosocial tension. Ideally, the individual must be able to achieve the positive value for each stage before proceeding to the next. If they are not able to achieve the suggested value, they can stay in that particular stage for a very long time. Or they can proceed to other stages, but they will exhibit behaviors that reflect poor coping behaviors. Their issues in the past will haunt them in the present and affect future behaviors. For example, if you were not able to achieve a healthy sense of trust during the infancy stage, you will still progress to the different stages, but you will have difficulty trusting other people. This can be reflected in behaviors such as being too suspicious or not being too expressive in terms of emotions because you don't trust others with your vulnerabilities. The tension is only resolved when you confront the issue actively.

But new interpretations of Erikson's theory reject this rigid model of progression only with the achievement of the values. Some psychologists are saying that we live with these tensions all of our lives. Even if we can resolve a particular issue in the past, we may encounter future circumstances wherein these values are going to be tested. For example, you may have achieved a good sense of autonomy in your early childhood stage. Years ahead, you may already be working in an office and you might encounter a situation where you will be faced with the same dilemma of a choice between being autonomous or guilty. Achieving the value of autonomy in the past increases your chances of achieving it at another time. But it also does not prevent you from regressing into guilt. Hence, these stages are not to be seen as rigid and fixed, but more fluid and dynamic. These issues will be present all our lives. But a good foundation in childhood will allow individuals to make better decisions in the future.

Virtues

Aside from the resolution of the tensions in each psychosocial stage, an individual will also gain a particular virtue. These virtues are enduring values one gains aside from choosing the positive value of each stage. They are not just extra values gained from successful resolution, but they are essential to the development of humans. They help us function better in our work and relationships. These virtues have an enduring quality that helps individuals resolve particular tensions better. Here are the virtues to be gained from the resolution of each life stage.

- Infancy: Hope
- Early Childhood: Will
- Play Age: Purpose
- School Age: Competency
- Adolescence: Fidelity
- Young Adulthood: Love
- Adulthood: Care

tension? These are very important questions if we want to compare how we are faring. But they are also very subjective, analyzed only from the point of view of the child or the caregivers. The validity of the theory then remains to be settled.

Nonetheless, these critiques will only enhance the truth of these psychosocial stages. The challenge now is really to apply these abstract concepts to real-life situations. It is good to have this theory as a guide in understanding the many issues we face in each developmental stage and therefore in the growth of an HSC.

But applying Erikson's theories in real life will definitely help us understand our particular situation and guide us into concrete steps to resolve these issues. What this book has tried to do is help parents understand what their highly sensitive child is experiencing and how they can triumph over conflicts.

Conclusion

I hope this book will be of help to all parents who want to understand their child and help him by giving him all their support and the necessary tools to live a childhood and adolescence in serenity because a peaceful child will be a strong and aware adult.

Highly sensitive children are therefore not only introverted, but they are also often creative, intuitive, artistic, and "spiritual".

Highly sensitive children may also have depression more easily, they also are more likely to have anxiety disorders. But while often a source of concern for parents, this trait is not necessarily inherently problematic. People have a tremendously wide range of sensitivities.

It's what you do with it that matters.

But once more, I underscore that all children will have certain challenges regardless of whether it is HSC or not. There is no perfect kid. What we have featured in this book are just some of the difficulties parents may experience when dealing with an HSC and the necessary information about how they can help their children overcome the challenges this trait imposes.

If you take away one thing from this book, it should be this: Your child is sensitive, so he needs to be confident and secure in who he is.

The parent's role is not just to reassure the child. The child also needs an open and honest conversation that explains what's going on for him, what's making him feel uncomfortable, and how he can do something about it.

This is the only way for them to develop the mental and emotional skills they need to handle feelings. The earlier you start talking with your child, the better.

Several personality traits can affect one's life later in life, sensitive temperament remains an important factor for predicting creative potential as well as overall happiness of adults. With this knowledge, we can see how being sensitive to others around us can be very beneficial to a child if they learn ways to deal with their sensitivity and self-regulate their emotions.

While most adults with HSC traits can keep their sensitivity under control, children and adolescents are still very much in the process of learning how to do so. The most important thing that can be done at this stage is to help a child learn that his or her sensitivity is not a bad thing and in fact, it is something he or she can use to their advantage!

Highly sensitive children do not necessarily have special gifts or talents. Most children of this type have bright futures ahead of them, just as most other children do. They simply may need a little more time and space to get used to their new surroundings as well as learn how to deal with overstimulation. This will help them become the exceptional people that they are capable of becoming once they have reached adulthood.

Thank you for reading This book.

If you enjoyed it please visit the site where you purchased it and write a brief review. Your feedback is important to me and will help other readers decide whether to read the book too.

Thank you!

Laura Henry

- Old Age: Wisdom

For example, a person in the young adulthood stage has to resolve the issue of intimacy vs. isolation. If she chooses to have a healthy sense of intimacy, then she also gains the virtue of love. Ultimately, these psychosocial stages help us to achieve these virtues to enable us to have richer relationships and to choose more mature and life-giving choices.

In the case of children, you have to set up an enabling environment for them to make these choices and achieve these virtues. You cannot make the choices for them. If they encounter a particular difficulty, they have to resolve that on their own. If they are having difficulty with school, you can help them but you cannot choose for them to achieve competency or industriousness. We can only provide the nurturing space with which they can make their own choices and resolve their particular psychosocial tension. They may not have full control of their feelings and behaviors as they are growing. But as parents, we can guide them to achieve these virtues. It will allow them to get well with their classmates, achieve in school, develop better communication skills and have a healthier disposition in life.

Criticism

Some critics of Erikson's theory of psychosocial development point out the lack of objective measures in defining the problems and the resolutions in each developmental stage. Critics find the theory inadequate in terms of specifying which particular events are necessary to illustrate the psychosocial tension in each stage and how we can claim that an individual has passed through each stage. This is a legitimate concern because our situations across cultures may be very different. For example, how can we say that a child can achieve trust and hope? Is it through giving them timely nourishment and stimulation? Is it measured in terms of frequency of feedings or the presence of a loving caregiver? When a child can work well with strangers, is that enough proof of the resolution of the psychosocial

Made in United States
North Haven, CT
11 October 2023